THE APOSTOLIC FATHERS

THE APOSTOLIC FATHERS

FOREWORD BY ❧ MARK GALLI

MOODY CLASSICS

MOODY PUBLISHERS
CHICAGO

2009 edition by
THE MOODY BIBLE INSTITUTE
OF CHICAGO

All Scripture quotations are taken from the King James Version.

Interior Design: Smartt Guys design
Cover Design: Kirk DouPonce / Dog Eared Design
Photo Credit: Bridgeman Art Library International
                PFA177659 Thirion: Triumph of Faith -Christian Martyrs in

Library of Congress Cataloging-in-Publication Data

The Apostolic Fathers.
  p. cm.
 ISBN 978-0-8024-5659-5
 1. Apostolic Fathers. 2. Fathers of the church. 3. Christian
literature, Early. I. Moody Publishers

BR63.A66 2009
270.1—dc22

                                    2009004791

We hope you enjoy this book from Moody Publishers. Our goal is to provide high-quality, thought-provoking books and products that connect truth to your real needs and challenges. For more information on other books and products written and produced from a biblical perspective, go to www.moodypublishers.com or write to:

Moody Publishers
820 N. LaSalle Boulevard
Chicago, IL 60610

1 3 5 7 9 10 8 6 4 2

Printed in the United States of America

CONTENTS

Foreword

by Mark Galli

NOW WHAT?

That question increasingly perplexed early Christians when, one by one, the original apostles began to die. By the time of the death of the last apostle, John (probably in Ephesus in the '90s), the church didn't have clear authoritative guidance from anyone who knew Jesus personally, and yet faced problems that threatened its survival.

Christians, for example, argued about the very person they worshipped each week. Some claimed that Jesus was divine, but denied His humanity: He just seemed to have human flesh; it just looked like He died. In reality, they said, He never participated in actual physical life. But if this were true, some asked, could we really count on our own bodily resurrection?

Christians also debated what a Christian lifestyle looked like. Some Jewish Christians, despite St. Paul's admonitions, insisted that Jewish religious laws still applied. Others lived by grace and ignored religious laws altogether. Others still didn't think anything of mixing their new faith with their old religious practices—like pinching a little incense to Caesar to keep the authorities happy.

Some churches were plagued by political strife. In Corinth in the '90s, impatient younger men apparently tired of the church's conservative ways. When they had had enough, they ousted their elders and took over the church. (Church politics is not a new problem!)

On top of all this, a widespread discouragement permeated this generation of Christians. Many believed they lacked moral focus. They weren't as fervent as the first Christians. They appeared indifferent about sexual purity, to holding their tongues or tempers, to treating one another with kindness, or to practicing self-control—to name a few concerns.

Without the twelve apostles to guide and admonish Christians about such matters, what was the early church to do?

Well, as we do today when we face hard issues, early Christians prayed and read Scripture. They also preached and published. And what you have in your hand is a modern translation of some early Christian publications. They include letters, a published sermon, moral guides, and what may be the earliest example of Christian fiction.

The early Christian revered these documents. They were like the best sellers of our day—publications everyone talked about. Some Christians, in fact, believed that documents like the Pastor of Hermas and 1 Clement ranked up there with the letters of Paul or the Gospels. It took a couple of centuries before the church sorted out secondary works (these) from primary (what we now call the New Testament). Yet even those who didn't think of these as "Scripture" viewed them as many today view the works of C. S. Lewis or Beth Moore or Rick Warren. Early Christians returned to these writings time and again for instruction and inspiration.

When you begin reading them, don't be surprised if you feel yourself entering another world—you are. Some things you will recognize immediately—their love of Jesus, their desire to do good works, their admonitions to one another to stay faithful to the gospel. But there is a lot that will seem odd—talk of traveling prophets (the Didache), visions of old women and haphazard building projects (Pastor of Hermas), and the use mythical stories to prove the resurrection (1 Clement)!

In particular, many modern readers balk at the ethical tone of these writings. Some call it moralistic; others "works righteousness." There isn't as much talk of grace and justification by faith as we would hope to find here.

There may be something to that. Every generation of Christians is tempted to turn faith into works. When the gospel seems too good to be true, we try to earn God's favor instead of simply receiving it as a gift. Still, I prefer to give these documents a charitable reading. I find in them enough references to God's mercy in Christ to make me think these early Christians were grounded in grace. No, the problem at the time was not salvation by grace but confusion about what it meant to live the faith day to day. To put it another way, think of these documents as extended expositions of James's reminder that faith without works is dead (2:20).

That being said, you're not holding Scripture here. These writings sometimes cross theological boundaries set by the New Testament. They can be "perfectionist" in the worst sense of that word, teaching that one can lead a nearly sinless life. Some passages do smack of salvation by works. And the Pastor of Hermas introduces a heresy about the incarnation, implying that Jesus was adopted as God's Son after living a perfect life in the Spirit!

So we should read these documents, as we read any non-biblical document, in light of the teaching of Holy Scripture. Then we can separate more easily the wheat from the chaff, and writings eighteen centuries old can still edify us today.

1 Clement

This is a letter from Clement, a foreign secretary in the church of Rome (and perhaps later the leading bishop of Rome), to the church at Corinth. He wrote it in AD 96 or 97, just after a persecution in Rome. Young leaders in Corinth had deposed their ruling elders—apparently the factious nature of that church had not changed much since Paul's day! Clement admonishes the church to moral purity and instructs it to respect validly instituted church order.

Clement knows Paul's Corinthian correspondence, as well as other first-century writings we now know as Scripture. But he works hard to adapt his message to the culture: he does not hesitate to use Stoic philosophy or ancient myths to drive home his points.

2 Clement

This is the earliest Christian sermon we have a copy of. It dates from somewhere between AD 98 and 170, and though named for Clement, we actually do not know who the author is exactly. He is a presbyter (elder) of a church, possibly in Alexandria, Egypt, or Corinth. In some ways, it reads like a "revival sermon," calling hearers to repent in light of the coming judgment. The audience seems to be mostly Gentile Christians who are attracted to Gnostic teachings, which denied the reality of Christ's incarnation and bodily resurrection.

One interesting historical note: This is the earliest historical document in which one of the Gospels is called "Scripture" (see 2:4).

The Letters of Ignatius

Ignatius had not been bishop of Antioch in Syria for long before authorities bound him in chains for his faith. Soldiers escorted him to Rome, possibly for trial but certainly for execution. Along the way, his military escort allowed him to visit churches. At two stops, he wrote to churches in what today is called Turkey.

Ignatius emphasized three things in these letters, which in some ways are his "last will and testament." First, he looks forward to his approaching martyrdom, and sees it as a way of sharing in Christ's sufferings (cf. Philippians 3:10).

Second, he promotes church unity—Corinth wasn't the only congregation of that era tempted by schism. To foster unity, he asks church members, as did Clement, to respect the authority of church leaders, especially the local bishop. He sees the local bishop as a representative of Christ himself.

Third, Ignatius responds to two false teachings. First, Jewish legalism, as noted above. Second, Docetism or Gnosticism (which denied that Jesus took on human flesh). Many Greco-Roman religions taught that matter was inherently evil, and Christians who came out of this background found it hard to believe in Jesus' real humanity.

These letters still vibrate with Ignatius's intense devotion to Christ, for whom he died somewhere between AD 98 and 117.

Letter of Polycarp to the Philippians

Polycarp was a bishop in Smyrna, just thirty-five miles north of Ephesus. Ignatius had written him a letter (included in the letters above) just a few months or years before he penned this letter to the Christians at Philippi.

The church there had sought his advice on a number of matters, one of which had to do with a presbyter named Valens. Apparently he had done something unethical regarding money. Polycarp wisely seeks Valens's repentance while encouraging the church to remain compassionate.

Polycarp comes across as a simple, humble, and direct man,

with no signs of pretension. He wrote this letter when he was in his forties, and already he shows signs of the man who would become famous as a martyr of the faith some forty years later.

The Martyrdom of Polycarp

This document stands as the oldest martyr account outside the pages of the New Testament. Formally, it claims to be a letter from the church at Smyrna (in particular, by one Marcion, whom we know nothing about) to the church in Philomelium (about five hundred miles inland in Turkey). It was written probably not long after Polycarp's death, which likely occurred sometime in the 150s (though some scholars date it a decade or two later).

The letter instructs readers to honor martyrs like Polycarp (with annual feasts, for example—see 18:3). It also encourages readers to hold firm to the faith in the face of increasing pressure to participate in the cult of the Roman state. This account was a model for later martyr stories, which became increasingly fanciful. Marcion restrains himself in the telling, and scholars believe it provides a generally reliable account of the courageous Polycarp's last hours.

In addition, one epilogue gives a brief account of how Polycarp dealt with the heretic Marcion on one visit to Rome (23:2–3). He was not a man who had much patience with false teaching!

Didache

The Didache (which means "teaching") is a manual of church discipline. Some scholars believe it came from the mid-first century, but most place it mid-to-late second century. Still, it harkens to an earlier time, giving us a glimpse into church life from the middle of first century Egypt or Syria.

The first part contains moral admonitions, presented as a choice between two ways, the way of life and the way of death. Reading between the lines, the modern reader can discern the moral challenges that early Christians faced, many of which sound familiar. Note for example the teaching about abortion (2:2).

The second part addresses specific pastoral issues, giving guidance on baptism, fasting, the Lord's Supper, itinerant prophets, and church order.

The Pastor of Hermas

Composed in Rome between AD 139 and 155, this document contains a number of visions and their explanations. According to the introduction, they were received by a servant or slave named Hermas, to whom a shepherd-like angel appeared. The work contains three parts: Visions (and their meaning), Commandments, and Similitudes (parables or examples).

This has similarities to the book of Revelation, but it contains much more overt teaching. The author has a high view of the church, and he tries to help the church deal with sin that occurs after baptism—which in his view cleanses recipients from sin. While it makes room for post-baptismal repentance, its teaching remains severe: "If any one is tempted by the devil, and sins after that great and holy calling in which the Lord has called

His people to everlasting life, he has opportunity to repent but once. But if he should sin frequently after this, and then repent, to such a man his repentance will be of no avail; for with difficulty will he live" (Book 2, Mandate 2, Chapter 3).

Its many and varied moral admonitions show, again, that many Christians in early Rome worried deeply about the lifestyle of believers.

The detailed visions suggest that the Pastor of Hermas was likely an early form of "teaching fiction," on the order of *Pilgrim's Progress* and other allegories. It was certainly as popular and as controversial in its day as various works are in ours.

* * *

Through these and other works of the first two centuries, we see early Christians grappling with their turbulent times. These documents refer often to the Gospels and the Epistles, which shows that early Christians looked for guidance to Holy Scripture, both the Old Testament and the recently written New Testament. In the end, it was that dependence, along with the promise of Jesus (Matthew 16:18), and the ministry of the Holy Spirit (working through documents like these, even with sometimes flawed teachings) that saw the church through these perilous times.

> MARK GALLI
> Senior Managing Editor, *Christianity Today*

The Letter of the Church of Rome to the Church of Corinth, Commonly Called Clement's First Letter

∾

THE TEXT

THE CHURCH OF GOD, living in exile in Rome, to the church of God, exiled in Corinth—to you who are called and sanctified by God's will through our Lord Jesus Christ. Abundant grace and peace be yours from God Almighty through Jesus Christ.

1 Due, dear friends, to the sudden and successive misfortunes and accidents we have encountered, we have, we admit, been rather long in turning our attention to your quarrels. We refer to the abominable and unholy schism, so alien and foreign to those whom God has chosen, which a few impetuous and headstrong fellows have fanned to such a pitch of insanity that your good name, once so famous and dear to us all, has fallen into the gravest ill repute. [2]Has anyone, indeed, stayed with you without attesting the excellence and firmness of your faith? without admiring your sensible and considerate Christian piety? without broadcasting your spirit of unbounded hospitality? without praising your perfect and trustworthy knowledge? 3For you always acted without partiality and walked in God's laws. You obeyed your rulers and gave your elders the proper respect. You disciplined the minds of your young people in moderation and dignity. You instructed your women to do everything with a blameless and pure conscience, and to give their husbands the affection they should. You taught them, too, to abide by the rule of obedience and to run their homes with dignity and thorough discretion.

2 You were all humble and without any pretensions, obeying orders rather than issuing them, more gladly giving than receiving. Content with Christ's rations and mindful of them, you stored his words carefully up in your hearts and held his sufferings before your eyes. 2In consequence, you were all granted a profound and rich peace and an insatiable longing to do good, while the Holy Spirit was abundantly poured out on you all. 3You were full of holy counsels, and, with zeal for the good and devout confidence, you stretched out your hands to almighty God, beseeching him to have mercy should you involuntarily have fallen into any sin. 4Day and night you labored for the whole brotherhood, that by your pity and sympathy the sum of his elect might be saved. 5You were sincere and guileless and bore no grudges. 6All sedition and schism were an abomination to you. You wept for the faults of your neighbors, while you reckoned their shortcomings as your own. 7You never regretted all the good you did, being "ready for any good deed." Possessed of an excellent and devout character, you did everything in His fear. The commands and decrees of the Lord were engraven on the tablets of your heart.

3 You were granted great popularity and growing numbers, so that the word of Scripture was fulfilled: "My beloved ate and drank and filled out and grew fat and started to kick." ²From this there arose rivalry and envy, strife and sedition, persecution and anarchy, war and captivity. ³And so "the dishonored" rose up "against those who were held in honor," those of no reputation against the notable, the stupid against the wise, "the young against their elders." ⁴For this reason righteousness and peace are far from you, since each has abandoned the fear of God and grown purblind in his faith, and ceased to walk by the rules of his precepts or to behave in a way worthy of Christ. Rather does each follow the lusts of his evil heart, by reviving that wicked and unholy rivalry, by which, indeed, "death came into the world."

4 For Scripture runs thus: "And it happened after some days that Cain brought God a sacrifice from the fruits of the earth, while Abel made his offering from the first-born of the sheep and of their fat. ²And God looked with favor on Abel and on his gifts; but he did not heed Cain and his sacrifices. ³And Cain was greatly upset and his face fell. ⁴And God said to Cain, 'Why are you so upset, and why has your face fallen? If you have made a correct offering but not divided it correctly, have you not sinned? ⁵Keep quiet. Your brother will turn to you and you shall rule over him.'

⁶And Cain said to his brother Abel, 'Let us go into the field.' And it happened that while they were in the field Cain attacked his brother Abel and killed him."

⁷You see, brothers, rivalry and envy are responsible for fratricide. ⁸Because of rivalry our forefather Jacob fled from the presence of his brother Esau. ⁹It was rivalry that caused Joseph to be murderously persecuted and reduced to slavery. ¹⁰Rivalry forced Moses to flee from the presence of Pharaoh, the king of Egypt, when he heard his fellow clansman say: "Who made you a ruler or judge over us? Do you want to slay me as you did the Egyptian yesterday?" ¹¹By reason of rivalry Aaron and Miriam were excluded from the camp. ¹²Rivalry cast Dathan and Abiram alive into Hades because they revolted against Moses, God's servant. ¹³Because of rivalry David not only incurred the envy of foreigners but was even persecuted by Saul, the king of Israel.

5 But, passing from examples in antiquity, let us come to the heroes nearest our own times. Let us take the noble examples of our own generation. ²By reason of rivalry and envy the greatest and most righteous pillars [of the Church] were persecuted, and battled to the death. ³Let us set before our eyes the noble apostles: ⁴Peter, who by reason of wicked jealousy, not only once or twice but frequently endured suffering and thus, bearing his witness, went to the glorious place which he merited. ⁵By reason of rivalry and contention Paul showed how to win the prize for patient endurance. ⁶Seven times he was in chains; he was exiled, stoned, became a herald [of the gospel] in East and West, and won the noble renown which his faith merited. 7To the whole world he taught righteousness, and reaching the limits of the West he bore his witness before rulers. And so, released from this world, he was taken up into the holy place and became the greatest example of patient endurance.

6 To these men who lived such holy lives there was joined a great multitude of the elect who by reason of rivalry were the victims of many outrages and tortures and who became outstanding examples among us. 2By reason of rivalry women were persecuted in the roles of Danaids and Dircae. Victims of dreadful and blasphemous outrages, they ran with sureness the course of faith to the finish, and despite their physical weakness won a notable prize. 3It was rivalry that estranged wives from their husbands and annulled the saying of our father Adam, "This is now bone of my bone and flesh of my flesh." 4Rivalry and contention have overthrown great cities and uprooted mighty nations.

7 We are writing in this vein, dear friends, not only to admonish you but also to remind ourselves. For we are in the same arena and involved in the same struggle. 2Hence we should give up empty and futile concerns, and turn to the glorious and holy rule of our tradition. 3Let us note what is good, what is pleasing and acceptable to Him who made us. 4Let us fix our eyes on the blood of Christ and let us realize how precious it is to his Father, since it was poured out for our salvation and brought the grace of repentance to the whole world. 5Let us go through all the generations and observe that from one generation to another the

Master "has afforded and opportunity of repentance" to those who are willing to turn to him. 6Noah preached repentance and those who heeded him were saved. 7Jonah preached destruction to the Ninevites; and when they had repented of their sins, they propitiated God with their prayers and gained salvation despite the fact they were not God's people.

8 The ministers of God's grace spoke about repentance through the Holy Spirit, 2and the Master of the universe himself spoke of repentance with an oath: "For as I live, says the Lord, I do not desire the death of the sinner, but his repentance." 3He added, too, this generous consideration: "Repent, O house of Israel, of your iniquity. Say to the sons of my people, Should your sins reach from earth to heaven, and be redder than scarlet and blacker than sackcloth, and should you turn to me with your whole heart and say 'Father!' I will heed you as though you were a holy people." 4And in another place this is what he says: "Wash and become clean: rid your souls of wickedness before my eyes. Cease from your wickedness, learn to behave well, devote yourselves to justice, rescue the wronged, uphold the rights of the orphan and grant the widow justice. And come, let us reason together, says the Lord; and if your sins are like purple, I will make them white as snow, and if they are like scarlet, I will make them white as wool. And if you are willing and heed me, you shall eat the good things of the earth. But if you are unwilling and do not heed me, the sword shall devour you. For it is the mouth of the Lord that has spoken thus. 5Since, there, he wanted all those he loved to have an opportunity to repent, he confirmed this by his almighty will.

9 So, then, let us fall in with his magnificent and glorious intention, and let us prostrate ourselves before him as suppliants of his mercy and kindness. Let us turn to his compassion and give up useless ventures and strife, and rivalry that leads to death. ²Let us father our eyes on those who have served his magnificent glory to perfection. ³Let us take Enoch, for instance, who, because he proved upright by his obedience, was translated and never died. ⁴Noah proved faithful in his ministry and preached a new birth to the world. Through him, therefore, the Master saved those living creatures that entered peacefully into the ark.

10 Abraham, who was called "The Friend," proved faithful in obeying God's words. ²It was obedience which led him to quit his country, his kindred, and his father's house, so that by leaving a paltry country, a mean kindred, and an insignificant house, he might inherit God's promises. ³For he told him: "Depart from your country and from your kindred and from the house of your father, and go to a land which I will show you. And I will make you great among the nations and I will bless you and I will make your name great and you will be blessed. And I will bless those who bless you and curse those who curse you, and all the tribes of the earth will be blessed through you." ⁴And again, when he separated from Lot, God told him: "Lift up your eyes and from where you now are look to the North, the South, the East, and the West, for all the land that you see I will give you and your seed forever. 5And I will make your seed like the dust of the earth. If anybody can count the dust of the earth, then your seed will be counted." 6And again he says: "God led Abraham out and told him: Look up to heaven and count the stars, if you can. That is how numerous your seed will be! And Abraham believed God and this was put down to his credit as an upright deed." 7Because of his faith and hospitality a son was granted to him in his old age, and he obediently offered him as a sacrifice to God on one of the hills which he indicated.

11 Because of his hospitality and religious devotion, Lot was saved from Sodom, when the whole countryside was condemned to fire and brimstone. In that way the Master made it clear that he does not forsake those who put their hope on him, but delivers to punishment and torment those who turn away from him. 2Of this latter, to be sure, his wife became an example. After quitting the city with him, she changed her mind and fell out with him, with the result that she became a pillar of salt that exists to this day. In this way it was made evident to all that the double-minded and those who question God's power are condemned and become a warning to all generations.

12 Because of her faith and hospitality Rahab the harlot was saved. 2For when the spies were sent to Jericho by Joshua the son of Nun, the king of the land got to know that they had come to spy on his country. Consequently he sent out men to capture them, intending to arrest them and put them to death. 3The hospitable Rahab, however, took them in and hid them in a room upstairs under stalks of flax. ⁴When the king's men learned of it, they said to her: "The men who are spying on our country went into your house. Bring them out, for this is the king's command." But she at once answered, "The men you seek came into my house, but they immediately departed and are on their way," and she pointed in the opposite direction. ⁵And she said to the men: "I am absolutely certain that the Lord God is handing this country over to you; for fear and terror of you have fallen on all its people. When, therefore, you come to take it, rescue me and my father's house." ⁶And they said to her: "It shall be exactly as you say. When you learn of our approach, you shall gather together all your family under your roof and they shall be saved. But whoever is found outside the house will perish." ⁷And in addition they gave her a sign that she should hang a piece of scarlet from her house. By this they made it clear that it was by the blood of the Lord that redemption was going to come to all who believe in God and hope on him. ⁸You see, dear friends, that not only faith but prophecy as well is exemplified in this woman.

13 Let us then, brothers, be humble and be rid of all pretensions and arrogance and silliness and anger. Let us act as Scripture bids us, for the Holy Spirit says: "Let not the wise man boast of his wisdom or the strong man of his might or the rich man of his wealth. But let him that boasts boast of the Lord; and so he will seek Him out and act justly and uprightly." Especially let us recall the words of the Lord Jesus, which he uttered to teach considerateness and patience. ²For this is what he said: "Show mercy, that you may be shown mercy. Forgive, that you may be forgiven. As you behave to others, so they will behave to you. As you give, so will you get. As you judge, so you will be judged. As you show kindness, so will you receive kindness. The measure you give will be the measure you get." ³Let us firmly hold on to this commandment and these injunctions so that in our conduct we may obey his holy words and be humble. ⁴For Holy Scripture says, "On whom shall I look except on him who is humble and gentle and who trembles at my words?"

14 It is right, then, and holy, brothers, that we should obey God rather than follow those arrogant and disorderly fellows who take the lead in stirring up loathsome rivalry. ²For we shall incur no ordinary harm, but rather great danger, if we recklessly give ourselves over to the designs of men who launch out into strife and sedition to alienate us from what is right. ³Let us be kind to one another in line with the compassion and tenderness of him who created us. ⁴For it is written: "The kind shall inhabit the land, and the innocent shall be left upon it. But those who transgress shall be destroyed from off it." ⁵And again he says: "I saw an ungodly man exalted and elevated like the cedars of Lebanon. But I passed by and, look, he had vanished! And I searched for his place and could not find it. Maintain innocence and have an eye for uprightness, for a man of peace will have descendants."

15 Let us, then, attach ourselves to those who are religiously devoted to peace, and not to those who wish for it hypocritically. ²For somewhere it is said, "This people honors me with its lips, but its heart is far removed from me." ³And again, "They blessed with their mouth, but they cursed with their heart." ⁴And again it says: "They loved him with their mouth, but they lied to him with their tongue. Their heart was not straightforward with him, and they were not faithful to his covenant. ⁵Therefore let the deceitful lips that speak evil against the righteous be struck dumb." And again: "May the Lord destroy all deceitful lips and the tongue that boasts unduly and those who say, 'We will boast of our tongues; our lips are our own; who is Lord over us? ⁶Because of the wretchedness of the poor and the groans of the needy I will now arise, says the Lord. I will place him in safety: I will act boldly in his cause.'"

16 It is to the humble that Christ belongs, not to those who exalt themselves above his flock. ²The scepter of God's majesty, the Lord Jesus Christ, did not come with the pomp of pride or arrogance, though he could have done so. But he came in humility just as the Holy Spirit said of him. ³For Scripture reads: "Lord, who has believed what we heard? And to whom has the arm of the Lord been revealed? Before him we announced that he was like a child, like a root in thirsty ground. He has no comeliness or glory. We saw him, and he had neither comeliness nor beauty. But his appearance was ignominious, deficient when compared to man's stature. He was a man marred by stripes and toil, and experienced in enduring weakness. Because his face was turned away, he was dishonored and disregarded. ⁴He it is who bears our sins and suffers pain for us. And we regarded him as subject to toil and stripes and affliction. [5]But it was for our sins that he was wounded and for our transgressions that he suffered. To bring us peace he was punished: by his stripes we were healed. [6]Like sheep we have all gone astray: each one went astray in his own way. [7]And the Lord delivered him up for our sins; and he does not open his mouth because he is abused. Like a sheep he is led off to be slaughtered; and just as a lamb before its shearers is dumb, so he does not open his mouth. In his humiliation his condemnation ended. [8]Who shall tell about his posterity? For his life was taken away from the earth. [9]Because of the transgressions of my people he came to his death. [10]And I will give the wicked as an offering for his burial and the rich for his death. For he did no iniquity and no deceit was found in his mouth. And the Lord's will is to cleanse him of his stripes. [11]If you make an offering for sin, your soul will see a long-lived posterity. [12]And the Lord's will is to do away with the toil of his soul, to show him light and to form him with understanding, to justify an upright man who serves many well. And he himself will bear their sins. [13]For this reason he shall have many heirs and he shall share the spoils of the strong, because his life was delivered up to death and he was reckoned among transgressors. [14]And he it was who bore the sins of many and was delivered up because of their sins.

[15]And again he himself says: "I am a worm and not a man, a disgrace to mankind and despised by the people. [16]All those who saw me mocked me, they made mouths at me and shook their heads, saying: 'He hoped on the Lord. Let him rescue him, let him

save him, since he is pleased with him!' ¹⁷"You see, dear friends, the kind of example we have been given. And so, if the Lord humbled himself in this way, what should we do who through him have come under the yoke of his grace?

17 Let us be imitators even of those who wandered around "in the skins of goats and sheep," and preached the coming of the Christ. We refer to the prophets Elijah and Elisha—yes, and Ezekiel, too—and to the heroes of old as well. ²Abraham was widely renowned and called the Friend of God. When he gazed on God's glory, he declared in his humility, "I am only dust and ashes." ³This is what is written about Job: "Job was an upright and innocent man, sincere, devout, and one who avoided all evil. ⁴But he was his own accuser when he said, "There is none who is free from stain, not even if his life lasts but a single day." ⁵Moses was called "faithful in all God's house" and God used him to bring His judgment on Egypt with scourges and torments. Yet even he, despite the great glory he was given, did not boast; but when he was granted an oracle from the bush, said: "Who am I that you send me? I have a feeble voice and a slow tongue." ⁶And again he says, "I am but steam from a pot."

18 And what shall we say of the famous David? God said of him, "I have discovered a man after my own heart, David the son of Jesse: I have anointed him with eternal mercy. ²But he too says to God: "Have mercy upon me, O God, according to your great mercy; and according to the wealth of your compassion wipe out my transgression. ³Wash me thoroughly from my iniquity and cleanse me from my sin, for I acknowledge my transgression and my sin is ever before me. ⁴Against you only have I sinned; and I have done evil in your sight. The result is that you are right when you speak and are acquitted when you are judged. ⁵For, see, I was conceived in iniquity, and in sin did my mother bear me. ⁶For, see, you have loved the truth: you have revealed to me the mysteries and secrets of your wisdom. ⁷You shall sprinkle me with hyssop and I shall be cleansed. You shall wash me and I shall be whiter than snow. ⁸You will make me hear joy and gladness: the bones which have been humbled shall rejoice. ⁹Turn your face from my sins and wipe away all my iniquities. ¹⁰Create in me a pure heart, O God, and renew a right spirit in my very core. ¹¹Cast me not away from your presence, and do not take your Holy Spirit away from me. ¹²Give me back the gladness of your salvation, and strengthen me with your guiding spirit. ¹³I will teach your ways to the wicked, and the godless shall turn back to you. ¹⁴Save me from bloodguiltiness, O God, the God of my salvation. ¹⁵My tongue will rejoice in your righteousness. You will open my mouth, O Lord, and my lips will proclaim your praise. ¹⁶For if you had wanted sacrifice, I would have given it. You will not find pleasure in burnt offerings. ¹⁷The sacrifice for God is a broken spirit: a broken and a humbled heart, O God, you will not despise."

19 The humility and obedient submissiveness of so many and so famous heroes have improved not only us but our fathers before us, and all who have received His oracles in fear and sincerity. [2]Since, then, we have benefited by many great and glorious deeds, let us run on to the goal of peace, which was handed down to us from the beginning. Let us fix our eyes on the Father and Creator of the universe and cling to his magnificent and excellent gifts of peace and kindness to us. [3]Let us see him in our minds and look with the eyes of our souls on his patient purpose. Let us consider how free he is from anger toward his whole creation.

20 The heavens move at his direction and peacefully obey him. [2]Day and night observe the course he has appointed them, without getting in each other's way. [3]The sun and the moon and the choirs of stars roll on harmoniously in their appointed courses at his command, and with never a deviation. [4]By his will and without dissension or altering anything he has decreed the earth becomes fruitful at the proper seasons and brings forth abundant food for men and beasts and every living thing upon it. [5]The unsearchable, abysmal depths and the indescribable regions of the underworld are subject to the same decrees. [6]The basin of the boundless sea is by his arrangement constructed to hold the heaped up waters, so that the sea does not flow beyond the barriers surrounding it, but does just as he bids it. [7]For he said, "Thus far you shall come, and your waves shall break within you." [8]The ocean which men cannot pass, and the worlds beyond it, are governed by the same decrees of the Master. [9]The seasons, spring, summer, autumn, and winter, peacefully give way to each other. [10]The winds from their different points perform their service at the proper time and without hindrance. Perennial springs, created for enjoyment and health, never fail to offer their life-giving breasts to men. The tiniest creatures come together in harmony and peace. [11]All these things the great Creator and Master of the universe ordained to exist in peace and harmony. Thus, he showered his benefits on them all, but most abundantly on us who have taken refuge in his compassion through our Lord Jesus Christ, [12]to whom be glory and majesty forever and ever Amen.

21 Take care, dear friends, that his many blessings do not turn out to be our condemnation, which will be the case if we fail to live worthily of him, to act in concert, and to do what is good and pleasing to him. [2]For he says somewhere, "The Spirit of the Lord is a lamp which searches the hidden depths of the heart." [3]Let us realize how near he is, and that none of our thoughts or of the ideas we have escapes his notice. [4]It is right, therefore, that we should not be deserters disobeying his will. [5]Rather than offend God, let us offend foolish and stupid men who exalt themselves and boast with their pretensions to fine speech. [6]Let us reverence the Lord Jesus Christ whose blood was given for us. Let us respect those who rule over us. Let us honor our elders. Let us rear the young in the fear of God. Let us direct our women to what is good. [7]Let them show a purity of character we can admire. Let them reveal a genuine sense of modesty. By their reticence let them show that their tongues are considerate. Let them not play favorites in showing affection, but in holiness let them love all equally, who fear God. [8]Let our children have a Christian training. Let them learn the value God sets on humility, what power pure love has with him, how good and excellent it is to fear him, and how this means salvation to everybody who lives in his fear with holiness and a pure conscience. [9]For he is the searcher of thoughts and of desires. It is his breath which is in us; and when he wants to, he will take it away.

22 Now Christian faith confirms all this. For this is how Christ addresses us through his Holy Spirit: "Come, my children, listen to me. I will teach you the fear of the Lord. [2]What man is there that desires life, and loves to see good days? [3]Keep your tongue from evil and your lips from uttering deceit. [4]Refrain from evil and do good. [5]Seek peace and follow after it. [6]The eyes of the Lord are over the upright and his ears are open to their petitions. But the face of the Lord is turned against those who do evil, to eradicate their memory from the earth. [7]The upright man cried out and the Lord heeded him and delivered him out of all his troubles. [8]Manifold are the plagues of the sinner, but his mercy will enfold those who hope on the Lord.

23 The all-merciful and beneficent Father has compassion on those who fear him, and with kindness and love he grants his favors to those who approach him with a sincere heart. [2]For this reason we must not be double-minded, and our souls must not harbor wrong notions about his excellent and glorious gifts. [3]Let that verse of Scripture be remote from us, which says: "Wretched are the double-minded, those who doubt in their soul and say, 'We have heard these things even in our fathers' times, and, see, we have grown old and none of them has happened to us.' [4]You fools! Compare yourselves to a tree. Take a vine: first it sheds its leaves, then comes a bud, then a leaf, then a flower, and after this a sour grape, and finally a ripe bunch." You note that the fruit of the tree reaches its maturity in a short time. 5So, to be sure, swiftly and suddenly his purpose will be accomplished, just as Scripture, too, testifies: "Quickly he will come and not delay, and the Lord will come suddenly into his temple, even the Holy One whom you expect.

24 Let us consider, dear friends, how the Master continually points out to us that there will be a future resurrection. Of this he made the Lord Jesus Christ the first fruits by raising him from the dead. 2Let us take note, dear friends, of the resurrection at the natural seasons. 3Day and night demonstrate resurrection. Night passes and day comes. Day departs and night returns. 4Take the crops as examples. How and in what way is the seeding done? 5The sower goes out and casts each of his seeds in the ground. When they fall on the ground they are dry and bare, and they decay. But then the marvelous providence of the Master resurrects them from their decay, and from a single seed many grow and bear fruit.

25 Let us note the remarkable token which comes from the East, from the neighborhood, that is, of Arabia. 2There is a bird which is called a phoenix. It is the only one of its kind and lives five hundred years. When the time for its departure and death draws near, it makes a burial nest for itself from frankincense, myrrh, and other spices; and when the time is up, it gets into it and dies. ³From its decaying flesh a worm is produced, which is nourished by the secretions of the dead creature and grows wings. When it is full-fledged, it takes up the burial nest containing the bones of its predecessor, and manages to carry them all the way from Arabia to the Egyptian city called Heliopolis. ⁴ And in broad daylight, so that everyone can see, it lights at the altar of the sun and puts them down there, and so starts home again. ⁵The priests then look up their dated records and discover it has come after a lapse of five hundred years.

26 Shall we, then, imagine that it is something great and surprising if the Creator of the universe raises up those who have served him in holiness and in the assurance born of a good faith, when he uses a mere bird to illustrate the greatness of his promise? ²For he says somewhere: "And you shall raise me up and I shall give you thanks" and, "I lay down and slept: I rose up because you are with me." ³And again Job says, "And you will make this flesh of mine, which has endured all this, to rise up."

27 With this hope, then, let us attach ourselves to him who is faithful to his promises and just in his judgments. ²He who bids us to refrain from lying is all the less likely to lie himself. For nothing is impossible to God save lying. ³Let us, then, rekindle our faith in him, and bear in mind that nothing is beyond his reach. ⁴By his majestic word he established the universe, and by his word he can bring it to an end. ⁵"Who shall say to him, What have you done? Or who shall resist his mighty strength?" He will do everything when he wants to and as he wants to. And not one of the things he has decreed will fail. 6Everything is open to his sight and nothing escapes his will. 7For "the heavens declare God's glory and the sky proclaims the work of his hands. Day pours forth words to day; and night imparts knowledge to night. And there are neither words nor speech, and their voices are not heard."

28 Since, then, he sees and hears everything, we should fear him and rid ourselves of wicked desires that issue in base deeds. By so doing we shall be sheltered by his mercy from the judgments to come. 2For where can any of us flee to escape his mighty hand? What world is there to receive anyone who deserts him? 3For Scripture says somewhere: "Where shall I go and where shall I hide from your presence? If I go up to heaven, you are there. If I go off to the ends of the earth, there is your right hand. If I make my bed in the depths, there is your spirit." 4Where, then, can anyone go or where can he flee to escape from him who embraces everything?

29 We must, then, approach him with our souls holy, lifting up pure and undefiled hands to him, loving our kind and compassionate Father, who has made us his chosen portion. 2For thus it is written: "When the Most High divided the nations, when he dispersed the sons of Adam, he fixed the boundaries of the nations to suit the number of God's angels. The Lord's portion became his people, Jacob: Israel was the lot that fell to him." 3And in another place it says: "Behold, the Lord takes for himself a people from among the nations, just as a man takes the first fruits of his threshing floor; and the Holy of Holies shall come forth from that nation."

30 Since, then, we are a holy portion, we should do everything that makes for holiness. We should flee from slandering, vile and impure embraces, drunkenness, rioting, filthy lusts, detestable adultery, and disgusting arrogance. 2"For God," says Scripture, "resists the arrogant, but gives grace to the humble." 3We should attach ourselves to those to whom God's grace has been given. We should clothe ourselves with concord, being humble, self-controlled, far removed from all gossiping and slandering, and justified by our deeds, not by words. 4For it says: "He who talks a lot will hear much in reply. Or does the prattler imagine he is right? 5Blessed is the one his mother bore to be short-lived. Do not indulge in talking overmuch." 6We should leave God to praise us and not praise ourselves. For God detests self-praisers.7Let others applaud our good deeds, as it was with our righteous forefathers. 8Presumption, audacity, and recklessness are traits of those accursed by God. But considerateness, humility, and modesty are the traits of those whom God has blessed.

31 Let us, then, cling to his blessing and note what leads to it. 2Let us unfold the tale of the ancient past. Why was our father Abraham blessed? Was it not because he acted in righteousness and truth, prompted by faith? 3Isaac, fully realizing what was going to happen, gladly let himself be led to sacrifice. 4In humility Jacob quit his homeland because of his brother. He went to

Laban and became his slave, and to him there were given the twelve scepters of the tribes of Israel.

32 And if anyone will candidly look into each example, he will realize the magnificence of the gifts God gives. ²For from Jacob there came all the priests and the Levites who serve at God's altar. From him comes the Lord Jesus so far as his human nature goes. From him there come the kings and rulers and governors of Judah. Nor is the glory of the other tribes derived from him insignificant. For God promised that "your seed shall be as the stars of heaven." ³So all of them received honor and greatness, not through themselves or their own deeds or the right things they did, but through his will. ⁴And we, therefore, who by his will have been called in Jesus Christ, are not justified of ourselves or by our wisdom or insight or religious devotion or the holy deeds we have done from the heart, but by that faith by which almighty God has justified all men from the very beginning. To him be glory forever and ever. Amen.

33 What, then, brothers, ought we to do? Should we grow slack in doing good and give up love? May the Lord never permit this to happen at any rate to us! Rather should we be energetic in doing "every good deed" with earnestness and eagerness. ²For the Creator and Master of the universe himself rejoices in his works. ³Thus by his almighty power he established the heavens and by his inscrutable wisdom he arranged them. He separated the land from the water surrounding it and fixed it upon the sure foundation of his own will. By his decree he brought into existence the living creatures which roam on it; and after creating the sea and the creatures which inhabit it, he fixed its boundaries by his power. 4Above all, with his holy and pure hands he fonned man, his outstanding and greatest achievement, stamped with his own image. 5For this is what God said: "Let us make man in our own image and likeness. And God made man: male and female he created." 6And so, when he had finished all this, he praised it and blessed it and said, "Increase and multiply." 7We should observe that all the righteous have been adorned with good deeds and the very Lord adorns himself with good deeds and rejoices. 8Since, then, we have this example, we should unhesitatingly give ourselves to his will, and put all our effort into acting uprightly.

34 The good laborer accepts the bread he has earned with his head held high; the lazy and negligent workman cannot look his employer in the face. 2We must, then, be eager to do good; for everything comes from Him. 3For he warns us: "See, the Lord is coming. He is bringing his reward with him, to pay each one according to his work." 4He bids us, therefore, to believe on him with all our heart, and not to be slack or negligent in "every good deed." 5He should be the basis of our boasting and assurance. We should be subject to his will. We should note how the whole throng of his angels stand ready to serve his will. 6For Scripture says: "Ten thousand times ten thousand stood by him, and thousands of thousands ministered to him and cried out: Holy, holy, holy is the Lord of Hosts: all creation is full of his glory." 7We too, then, should gather together for worship in concord and mutual trust, and earnestly beseech him as it were with one mouth, that we may share in his great and glorious promises. 8For he says, "Eye has not seen and ear has not heard and man's heart has not conceived what he has prepared for those who patiently wait for him."

35 How blessed and amazing are God's gifts, dear friends! 2Life with immortality, splendor with righteousness, truth with confidence, faith with assurance, self-control with holiness! And all these things are within our comprehension. 3What, then, is being prepared for those who wait for him? The Creator and Father of eternity, the all-holy, himself knows how great and wonderful it is. 4We, then, should make every effort to be found in the number of those who are patiently looking for him, so that we may share in the gifts he has promised. 5And how shall this be, dear friends? If our mind is faithfully fixed on God; if we seek out what pleases and delights him; if we do what is in accord with his pure will, and follow in the way of truth. If we rid ourselves of all wickedness, evil, avarice, contentiousness, malice, fraud, gossip, slander, hatred of God, arrogance, pretension, conceit, and inhospitality. 6God hates those who act in this way; "and not only those who do these things but those who applaud them." 7For Scripture says: "But God told the sinner: Why do you speak of my statutes and have my covenant on your lips? 8You hated discipline and turned your back on my words. If you saw a thief you went along with him, and you threw in your lot with adulterers. Your mouth overflowed with iniquity, and your tongue wove deceit. You sat there slandering your brother and putting a stumbling block in the way of your mother's son. ⁹This you did, and I kept silent. You suspected, you wicked man, that I would be like you. ¹⁰I will reproach you and show you your very self. ¹¹Ponder, then, these things, you who forget God, lest he seize you like a lion and there be no one to save you. ¹²A sacrifice of praise will glorify me, and that is the way by which I will show him God's salvation."

36 This is the way, dear friends, in which we found our salvation, Jesus Christ, the high priest of our offerings, the protector and helper of our weakness. ²Through him we fix our gaze on the heights of heaven. In him we see mirrored God's pure and transcendent face. Through him the eyes of our hearts have been opened. Through him our foolish and darkened understanding springs up to the light. Through him the Master has willed that we should taste immortal knowledge. For, "since he reflects God's splendor, he is as superior to the angels as his title is more distinguished than theirs." ³For thus it is written: "He who makes his angels winds, and his ministers flames of fire."⁴But of his son this is what the Master said: "You are my son: today I have begotten you. Ask me and I will give you the nations for you to inherit, and the ends of the earth for you to keep. ⁵And again he says to him: "Sit at my right hand until I make your enemies your footstool." ⁶Who are meant by "enemies"? Those who are wicked and resist his will.

37 Really in earnest, then, brothers, we must march under his irreproachable orders. ²Let us note with what discipline, readiness, and obedience those who serve under our generals carry out orders. ³Not everybody is a general, colonel, captain, sergeant, and so on. But "each in his own rank" carries out the orders of the emperor and of the generals. ⁴The great cannot exist without the small; neither can the small exist without the great. All are linked together; and this has an advantage. ⁵Take our body, for instance. The head cannot get along without the feet. Nor, similarly, can the feet get along without the head. "The tiniest parts of our body are essential to it," and are valuable to the total body. Yes, they all act in concord, and are united in a single obedience to preserve the whole body.

38 Following this out, we must preserve our Christian body too in its entirety. Each must be subject to his neighbor, according to his special gifts. ²The strong must take care of the weak; the weak must look up to the strong. The rich must provide for the poor; the poor must thank God for giving him someone to meet his needs. The wise man must show his wisdom not in words but in good deeds. The humble must not brag about his humility; but should give others occasion to mention it. He who is continent must not put on airs. He must recognize that his self-control is a gift from another. ³We must take to heart, brothers, from what stuff we were created, what kind of creatures we were when we entered the world, from what a dark grave he who fashioned and created us brought us into his world. And we must realize the preparations he so generously made before we were born. ⁴Since, then, we owe all this to him, we ought to give him unbounded thanks. To him be glory forever and ever. Amen.

39 Thoughtless, silly, senseless, and ignorant folk mock and jeer at us, in an effort, so they imagine, to exalt themselves. ²But what can a mere mortal do? What power has a creature of earth? ³For it is written: "There was no shape before my eyes, but I heard a breath and a voice. ⁴What! Can a mortal be pure before the Lord? Or can a man be blameless for his actions, if he does not believe in His servants and finds something wrong with His angels? ⁵Not even heaven is pure in His sight: let alone those who live in houses of clay—of the very same clay of which we ourselves are made. He smites them like a moth; and they do not last from dawn to dusk. They perish, for they cannot help themselves. ⁶He breathes on them, and they die for lack of wisdom. ⁷Call out and see if anyone will heed you, or if you will see any of the holy angels. For wrath destroys a stupid man, and rivalry is the death of one in error. ⁸I have seen the foolish taking root, but suddenly their home is swept away. ⁹May their sons be far from safety! May they be mocked at the doors of lesser men, and there will be none to deliver them. For what has been prepared by them, the righteous will eat; and they shall not be delivered from troubles.

40 Now that this is clear to us and we have peered into the depths of the divine knowledge, we are bound to do in an orderly fashion all that the Master has bidden us to do at the proper times he set. ²He ordered sacrifices and services to be performed; and required this to be done, not in a careless and disorderly way, but at the times and seasons he fixed. ³Where he wants them performed, and by whom, he himself fixed by his supreme will, so that everything should be done in a holy way and with his approval, and should be acceptable to his will. ⁴Those, therefore, who make their offerings at the time set, win his approval and blessing. For they follow the Master's orders and do no wrong. ⁵The high priest is given his particular duties: the priests are assigned their special place, while on the Levites particular tasks are imposed. The layman is bound by the layman's code.

41 "Each of us," brothers, "in his own rank" must win God's approval and have a clear conscience. We must not transgress the rules laid down for our ministry, but must perform it reverently. ²Not everywhere, brothers, are the different sacrifices—the daily ones, the freewill offerings, and those for sins and trespasses— offered, but only in Jerusalem. And even there sacrifices are not made at any point, but only in front of the sanctuary, at the altar, after the high priest and the ministers mentioned have inspected the offering for blemishes. ³Those, therefore, who act in any way at variance with his will, suffer the penalty of death. ⁴You see, brothers, the more knowledge we are given, the greater risks we run.

42 The apostles received the gospel for us from the Lord Jesus Christ; Jesus, the Christ, was sent from God. ²Thus Christ is from God and the apostles from Christ. In both instances the orderly procedure depends on God's will. ³And so the apostles, after receiving their orders and being fully convinced by the resurrection of our Lord Jesus Christ and assured by God's word, went out in the confidence of the Holy Spirit to preach the good news that God's Kingdom was about to come. 4They preached in country and city, and appointed their first converts, after testing them by the Spirit, to be the bishops and deacons of future believers. 5Nor was this any novelty, for Scripture had mentioned bishops and deacons long before. For this is what Scripture says somewhere: "I will appoint their bishops in righteousness and their deacons in faith."

43 And is it any wonder that those Christians whom God had entrusted with such a duty should have appointed the officers mentioned? For the blessed Moses too, "who was a faithful servant in all God's house," recorded in the sacred books all the orders given to him, and the rest of the prophets followed in his train by testifying with him to his legislation. 2Now, when rivalry for the priesthood arose and the tribes started quarreling as to which of them should be honored with this glorious privilege, Moses bid the twelve tribal chiefs bring him rods, on each of which was written the name of one of the tribes. These he took and bound, sealing them with the rings of the tribal leaders; and he put them in the tent of testimony on God's table. 3Then he shut the tent and put seals on the keys just as he had on the rods. 4And he told them: "Brothers, the tribe whose rod puts forth buds is the one God has chosen for the priesthood and for his ministry." 5Early the next morning he called all Israel together, six hundred thousand strong, and showed the seals to the tribal chiefs and opened the tent of testimony and brought out the rods. And it was discovered that Aaron's rod had not only budded, but was actually bearing fruit. 6What do you think, dear friends? Did not Moses know in advance that this was going to happen? Why certainly. But he acted the way he did in order to forestall anarchy in Israel, and so that the name of the true and only God might be glorified. To Him be the glory forever and ever. Amen.

44 Now our apostles, thanks to our Lord Jesus Christ, knew that there was going to be strife over the title of bishop. 2It was for this reason and because they had been given an accurate knowledge of the future, that they appointed the officers we have mentioned. Furthermore, they later added a codicil to the effect that, should these die, other approved men should succeed to their ministry. 3In the light of this, we view it as a breach of justice to remove from their ministry those who were appointed either by them [i.e., the apostles] or later on and with the whole church's consent, by others of the proper standing, and who, long enjoying everybody's approval, have ministered to Christ's flock faultlessly, humbly, quietly, and unassumingly. 4For we shall be guilty of no slight sin if we eject from the episcopate men who have offered the sacrifices with innocence and holiness. 5Happy, indeed, are those presbyters who have already passed on, and who ended a life of fruitfulness with their task complete. For they need not fear that anyone will remove them from their secure positions. 6But you, we observe, have removed a number of people, despite their good conduct, from a ministry they have fulfilled with honor and integrity.

45 Your contention and rivalry, brothers, thus touches matters that bear on our salvation. 2You have studied Holy Scripture, which contains the truth and is inspired by the Holy Spirit. 3You realize that there is nothing wrong or misleading written in it. You will not find that upright people have ever been disowned by holy men. 4The righteous, to be sure, have been persecuted, but by wicked men. They have been imprisoned, but by the godless. They have been stoned by transgressors, slain by men prompted by abominable and wicked rivalry. 5Yet in such sufferings they bore up nobly. 6What shall we say, brothers? Was Daniel cast into a den of lions by those who revered God? 7Or was Ananias, Azarias, or Mishael shut up in the fiery furnace by men devoted to the magnificent arid glorious worship of the Most High? Not for a moment! Who, then, was it that did such things? Detestable men, thoroughly and completely wicked, whose factiousness drove them to such a pitch of fury that they tormented those who resolutely served God in holiness and innocence. They failed to realize that the Most High is the champion and defender of those who worship his excellent name with a pure conscience. To him be the glory forever and ever. Amen. 8But those who held out with confidence inherited glory and honor. They were exalted, and God inscribed them on his memory forever and ever. Amen.

46 Brothers, we must follow such examples. 2For it is written: "Follow the saints, because those who follow them will become saints." ³Again, it says in another place: "In the company of the innocent, you will be innocent; in the company of the elect, you will be elect; and in a crooked man's company you will go wrong." ⁴Let us, then, follow the innocent and the upright. They, it is, who are God's elect. ⁵Why is it that you harbor strife, bad temper, dissension, schism, and quarreling? ⁶Do we not have one God, one Christ, one Spirit of grace which was poured out on us? And is there not one calling in Christ? ⁷Why do we rend and tear asunder Christ's members and raise a revolt against our own body? Why do we reach such a pitch of insanity that we are oblivious of the fact we are members of each other? Recall the words of our Lord Jesus. ⁸For he said: "Woe to that man! It were better for him not to have been born than to be the occasion of one of my chosen ones stumbling. It were better for him to have a millstone around his neck and to be drowned in the sea, than to pervert one of my chosen." ⁹Your schism has led many astray; it has made many despair; it has made many doubt; and it has distressed us all. Yet it goes on!

47 Pick up the letter of the blessed apostle Paul. ²What was the primary thing he wrote to you, "when he started preaching the gospel?" ³To be sure, under the Spirit's guidance, he wrote to you about himself and Cephas and Apollos, because even then you had formed cliques. ⁴Factiousness, however, at that time was a less serious sin, since you were partisans of notable apostles and of a man they endorsed. ⁵But think now who they are who have led you astray and degraded your honorable and celebrated love of the brethren. [6]It is disgraceful, exceedingly disgraceful, and unworthy of your Christian upbringing, to have it reported that because of one or two individuals the solid and ancient Corinthian Church is in revolt against its presbyters. [7]This report, moreover, has reached not only us, but those who dissent from us as well. The result is that the Lord's name is being blasphemed because of your stupidity, and you are exposing yourselves to danger.

48 We must, then, put a speedy end to this. We must prostrate ourselves before the Master, and beseech him with tears to have mercy on us and be reconciled to us and bring us back to our honorable and holy practice of brotherly love. [2]For it is this which is the gate of righteousness, which opens the way to life, as it is written: "Open the gates of righteousness for me, so that I may enter by them and praise the Lord. [3]This is the Lord's gate: the righteous shall enter by it." [4]While there are many gates open, the gate of righteousness is the Christian gate. Blessed are all those who enter by it and direct their way "in holiness and righteousness," by doing everything without disorder. [5]Let a man be faithful, let him be capable of uttering "knowledge," let him be wise in judging arguments, let him be pure in conduct. [6]But the greater he appears to be, the more humble he ought to be, and the more ready to seek the common good in preference to his own.

49 Whoever has Christian love must keep Christ's commandments. [2]Who can describe the bond of God's love? [3]Who is capable of expressing its great beauty? 4The heights to which love leads are beyond description. 5Love unites us to God. "Love hides a multitude of sins." Love puts up with everything and is always patient. There is nothing vulgar about love, nothing arrogant. Love knows nothing of schism or revolt. Love does everything in harmony. By love all God's elect were made perfect. Without love nothing can please God. 6By love the Master accepted us. Because of the love he had for us, and in accordance with God's will, Jesus Christ our Lord gave his blood for us, his flesh for our flesh, and his life for ours.

50 You see, brothers, how great and amazing love is, and how its perfection is beyond description. 2Who is able to possess it save those to whom God has given the privilege? Let us, then, beg and implore him mercifully to grant us love without human bias and to make us irreproachable. 3All the generations from Adam to our day have passed away, but those who, by the grace of God, have been made perfect in love have a place among the saints, who will appear when Christ's Kingdom comes. 4For it is written: "Go into your closets for a very little while, until my wrath and anger pass, and I will remember a good day and I will raise you up from your graves." 5Happy are we, dear friends, if we keep God's commandments in the harmony of love, so that by love our sins may be forgiven us. 6For it is written: "Happy are those whose iniquities are forgiven and whose sins are covered. Happy is the man whose sin the Lord will not reckon, and on whose lips there is no deceit." 7This is the blessing which was given to those whom God chose through Jesus Christ our Lord. To him be the glory forever and ever. Amen.

51 Let us, then, ask pardon for our failings and for whatever we have done through the prompting of the adversary. And those who are the ringleaders of the revolt and dissension ought to reflect upon the common nature of our hope. ²Those, certainly, who live in fear and love would rather suffer outrages themselves than have their neighbors do so. They prefer to endure condemnation themselves rather than bring in reproach our tradition of noble and righteous harmony. ³It is better for a man to confess his sins than to harden his heart in the way those rebels against God's servant Moses hardened theirs. The verdict against them was made very plain. ⁴For "they went down to Hades alive," and "death will be their shepherd." Pharaoh and his host and all the princes of Egypt and "the chariots and their riders" were engulfed in the Red Sea and perished, for no other reason than that they hardened their foolish hearts after Moses, God's servant, had done signs and wonders in Egypt.

52 The Master, brothers, has no need of anything. He wants nothing of anybody save that he should praise him. ²For his favorite, David, says: "I will praise the Lord; and this will please him more than a young calf with horns and hoofs. Let the poor observe this and rejoice. ³And again he says: "Offer to God the sacrifice of praise, and pay your vows to the Most High. Call on me in the day of your affliction and I will rescue you, and you will glorify me. ⁴For the sacrifice God wants is a broken spirit."

53 You know the Holy Scriptures, dear friends—you know them well—and you have studied God's oracles. It is to remind you of them that we write the way we do. [2]When Moses ascended the mountain and spent forty days and forty nights in fasting and humiliation, God said to him: "Get quickly down from here, for your people, whom you led out of the land of Egypt, have broken the law. They have quickly turned from the way you bid them take. They have cast idols for themselves." [3]And the Lord told him: "I have spoken to you once, yes, twice, saying, I have looked at this people and, see, it is obstinate. Let me exterminate them, and I will wipe out their name from under heaven, and I will make you into a great and wonderful nation, much larger than this one." [4]And Moses answered: "No, no, Lord. Pardon my people's sin, or else eliminate me too from the roll of the living." [5]O great love! 0 unsurpassed perfection! The servant speaks openly to his Lord. He begs pardon for his people or requests that he too will be wiped out along with them.

54 Well, then, who of your number is noble, large-hearted, and full of love? [2]Let him say: "If it is my fault that revolt, strife, and schism have arisen, I will leave, I will go away wherever you wish, and do what the congregation orders. Only let Christ's flock live in peace with their appointed presbyters." [3]The man who does this will win for himself great glory in Christ; and will be welcome everywhere. "For the earth and its fullness belong to the Lord." [4]This has been the conduct and will always be the conduct of those who have no regrets that they belong to the city of God.

55 Let us take some heathen examples: In times of plague many kings and rulers, prompted by oracles, have given themselves up to death in order to rescue their subjects by their own blood. Many have quit their own cities to put an end to sedition. [2]We know many of our own number who have had themselves imprisoned in order to ransom others. Many have sold themselves into slavery and given the price to feed others. [3]Many women, empowered by God's grace, have performed deeds worthy of men. [4]The blessed Judith, when her city was under siege, begged of the elders to be permitted to leave it for the enemy's camp. [5]So she exposed herself to danger and for love of her country and of her besieged people, she departed. And the Lord delivered Holofernes into the hands of a woman. [6]To no less danger did Esther, that woman of perfect faith, expose herself in order to rescue the twelve tribes of Israel when they were on the point of being destroyed. For by her fasting and humiliation she implored the all-seeing Master, the eternal God; and he beheld the humility of her soul and rescued her people for whose sake she had faced danger.

56 So we too must intercede for any who have fallen into sin, that considerateness and humility may be granted to them and that they may submit, not to us, but to God's will. For in that way they will prove fruitful and perfect when God and the saints remember them with mercy. [2]We must accept correction, dear friends. No one should resent it. Warnings we give each other are good and thoroughly beneficial. For they bind us to God's will.

3This is what the Holy Word says about it: "The Lord has disciplined me severely and has not given me up to death. 4For the Lord disciplines the one he loves, and punishes every son he accepts." 5For, it says, "the upright man will discipline me with mercy and reprove me. But let not the oil of sinners anoint my head." 6And again it says: "Happy is the man the Lord reproves. Do not refuse the Almighty's warning. For he inflicts pain, and then makes all well again. 7He smites, but his hands heal. 8Six times will he rescue you from trouble; and on the seventh evil will not touch you. 9In famine he will rescue you from death; in war he will deliver you from the edge of the sword. 10From the scourge of the tongue he will hide you, and you will not be afraid of evils when they come. 11You will ridicule the wicked and lawless, and not be afraid of wild beasts; 12for wild beasts will leave you in peace. 13Then you will discover that your house will be peaceful, and the tent in which you dwell will be safe. 14You will find, too, that your seed will be numerous, and your children like the grass of the fields. 15You will come to your tomb like ripe wheat harvested at the appropriate season, or like a heap on the threshing floor gathered together at the right time. 16You see, dear friends, how well protected they are whom the Master disciplines. Yes, he is like a good Father, and disciplines us so that the outcome of his holy discipline may mean mercy for us.

57 And that is why you who are responsible for the revolt must submit to the presbyters. You must humble your hearts and be disciplined so that you repent. 2You must learn obedience, and be done with your proud boasting and curb your arrogant tongues. For it is better for you to have an insignificant yet creditable place in Christ's flock than to appear eminent and be excluded from Christ's hope. ³For this is what the excellent Wisdom says: "See, I will declare to you the utterance of my Spirit: I will teach you my word. ⁴Since I called and you did not listen, since I poured out words and you did not heed, but disregarded my plans and disobeyed my reproofs, therefore I will laugh at your destruction. And I will rejoice when ruin befalls you and when confusion suddenly overtakes you, and catastrophe descends like a hurricane, or when persecution and siege come upon you. ⁵Yes, it will be like this: when you call upon me, I will not heed you. The wicked shall look for me and shall not find me. For they detested wisdom, and did not choose the fear of the Lord. They had no desire to heed my counsels, and mocked at my reproofs. ⁶For this reason they shall eat the fruit of their ways and fill themselves with impiety. ⁷Because they wronged babes, they will be slain; and by being searched out the impious shall be destroyed. But he that listens to me will dwell in confident hope and live quietly, free from the fear of any misfortune."

58 So, then, let us obey his most holy and glorious name and escape the threats which Wisdom has predicted against the disobedient. In that way we shall live in peace, having our confidence in his most holy and majestic name. ²Accept our advice, and you will never regret it. For as God lives, and as the Lord Jesus Christ lives and the Holy Spirit (on whom the elect believe and hope), the man who with humility and eager considerateness and with no regrets does what God has decreed and ordered will be enlisted and enrolled in the ranks of those who are saved through Jesus Christ. Through him be the glory to God forever and ever. Amen.

59 If, on the other hand, there be some who fail to obey what God has told them through us, they must realize that they will enmesh themselves in sin and in no insignificant danger. ²We, for our part, will not be responsible for such a sin. But we will beg with earnest prayer and supplication that the Creator of the universe will keep intact the precise number of his elect in the whole world, through his beloved Child Jesus Christ. It was through him that he called us "from darkness to light," from ignorance to the recognition of his glorious name ³to hope on Your name, which is the origin of all creation. You have opened "the eyes of our hearts" so that we realize you alone are "highest among the highest, and ever remain holy among the holy?" "You humble the pride of the arrogant, overrule the plans of the nations, raise up the humble and humble the haughty. You make rich and make poor; you slay and bring to life; you alone are the guardian of spirits and the God of all flesh." You see into the depths: you look upon men's deeds; you aid those in danger and "save those in despair." You are the creator of every spirit and watch over them. You multiply the nations on the earth, and from out of them all you have chosen those who love you through Jesus Christ, your beloved Son.

Through him you have trained us, made us saints, and honored us.

4We ask you, Master, be our "helper and defender." Rescue those of our number in distress; raise up the fallen; assist the needy; heal the sick; turn back those of your people who stray; feed the hungry; release our captives; revive the weak; encourage those who lose heart. "Let all the nations realize that you are the only God," that Jesus Christ is your Child, and "that we are your people and the sheep of your pasture."

60 You brought into being the everlasting structure of the world by what you did. You, Lord, made the earth. You who are faithful in all generations, righteous in judgment, marvelous in strength and majesty, wise in creating, prudent in making creation endure, visibly good, kind to those who trust in you, "merciful and compassionate," —forgive us our sins, wickedness, trespasses, and failings. 2Do not take account of every sin of your slaves and slave girls, but cleanse us with the cleansing of your truth, and "guide our steps so that we walk with holy hearts and do what is good and pleasing to you" and to our rulers.

3Yes, Master, "turn your radiant face toward us" in peace, "for our good, that we may be shielded "by your powerful hand" and rescued from every sin "by your uplifted arm." 4Deliver us, too, from all who hate us without good reason. Give us and all who live on the earth harmony and peace, just as you did to our fathers when they reverently "called upon you in faith and truth." And grant that we may be obedient to your almighty and glorious name, and to our rulers and governors on earth.

61 You, Master, gave them imperial power through your majestic and indescribable might, so that we, recognizing it was you who gave them the glory and honor, might submit to them, and in no way oppose your will. Grant them, Lord, health, peace, harmony, and stability, so that they may give no offense in administering the government you have given them. [2]For it is you, Master, the heavenly "King of eternity," who give the sons of men glory and honor and authority over the earth's people. Direct their plans, O Lord, in accord with "what is good and pleasing to you," so that they may administer the authority you have given them, with peace, considerateness, and reverence, and so win your mercy. [3]We praise you, who alone are able to do this and still better things for us, through the high priest and guardian of our souls, Jesus Christ. Through him be the glory and the majesty to you now and for all generations and forevermore. Amen.

62 We have written enough to you, brothers, about what befits our religion and is most helpful to those who want reverently and uprightly to lead a virtuous life. [2]We have, indeed, touched on every topic—faith, repentance, genuine love, self-control, sobriety, and patience. We have reminded you that you must reverently please almighty God by your uprightness, truthfulness, and longsuffering. You must live in harmony, bearing no grudges, in love, peace, and true considerateness, just as our forefathers, whom we mentioned, won approval by their humble attitude to the Father, God the Creator, and to all men. [3]We were, moreover, all the more delighted to remind you of these things, since we well realized we were writing to people who were real believers and of the highest standing, and who had made a study of the oracles of God's teaching.

63 Hence it is only right that, confronted with such examples and so many of them, we should bow the neck and adopt the attitude of obedience. Thus, by giving up this futile revolt, we may be free from all reproach and gain the true goal ahead of us. ²Yes, you will make us exceedingly happy if you prove obedient to what we, prompted by the Holy Spirit, have written, and if, following the plea of our letter for peace and harmony, you rid yourselves of your wicked and passionate rivalry.

³We are sending you, moreover, trustworthy and discreet persons who from youth to old age have lived irreproachable lives among us. They will be witnesses to mediate between us. ⁴We have done this to let you know that our whole concern has been, and is, to have peace speedily restored among you.

64 And now may the all-seeing God and Master "of spirits" and Lord "of all flesh," who chose the Lord Jesus Christ and us through him "to be his own people," grant to every soul over whom His magnificent and holy name has been invoked, faith, fear, peace, patience, long-suffering, self-control, purity, and sobriety. So may we win his approval through our high priest and defender, Jesus Christ. Through him be glory, majesty, might, and honor to God, now and forevermore. Amen.

65 Be quick to return our delegates in peace and joy,

Claudius Ephebus and Valerius Bito, along with Fortunatus. In that way they will the sooner bring us news of that peace and harmony we have prayed for and so much desire, and we in turn will the more speedily rejoice over your healthy state.

The grace of our Lord Jesus Christ be with you and with all everywhere whom God has called through him. Through him be glory, honor, might, majesty, and eternal dominion to God, from everlasting to everlasting. Amen.

An Anonymous Sermon,
Commonly Called
Clement's Second Letter
to the Corinthians

∞

THE TEXT

1 Brothers, we ought to think of Jesus Christ as we do of God—as the "judge of the living and the dead." And we ought not to belittle our salvation. [2]For when we belittle him, we hope to get but little; and they that listen as to a trifling matter, do wrong. And we too do wrong when we fail to realize whence and by whom and into what circumstances we were called, and how much suffering Jesus Christ endured for us. [3]How, then, shall we repay him, or what return is worthy of his gift to us? How many blessings we owe to him! [4]For he has given us light; as a Father he has called us sons; he has rescued us when we were perishing. [5]How, then, shall we praise him, or how repay him for what we have received? [6]Our minds were impaired; we worshiped stone and wood and gold and silver and brass, the works of men; and our whole life was nothing else but death. So when we were wrapped in darkness and our eyes were full of such mist, by his will we recovered our sight and put off the cloud which infolded us. [7]For he took pity on us and in his tenderness saved us, since he saw our great error and ruin, and that we had no hope of salvation unless it came from him. [8]For he called us when we were nothing, and willed our existence from nothing.

2 "Rejoice, you who are barren and childless; cry out and shout, you who were never in labor; for the desolate woman has many more children than the one with the husband." When he says, "Rejoice, you who are barren and childless," he refers to us; for our Church was barren before it was given children. [2]And when he says, "Shout, you who were never in labor," this is what he means: we should offer our prayers to God with sincerity, and not lose heart like women in labor. [3]And he says, "The desolate woman has many more children than the one with the husband," because our people seemed to be abandoned by God. But now that we believe, we have become more numerous than those who seemed to have God. [4]And another Scripture says, "I did not come to call the righteous, but sinners." [5]This means that those perishing must be saved. [6]Yes, a great and wonderful thing it is to support, not things which are standing, but those which are collapsing. [7]Thus it was that the Christ willed to save what was perishing; and he saved many when he came and called us who were actually perishing.

3 Seeing, then, that he has had such pity on us, firstly, in that we who are alive do not sacrifice to dead gods or worship them, but through him have come to know the Father of truth—what is knowledge in reference to him, save refusing to deny him through whom we came to know the Father? 2He himself says, "He who acknowledges me before men, I will acknowledge before my Father." 3This, then, is our reward, if we acknowledge him through whom we are saved. 4But how do we acknowledge him? By doing what he says and not disobeying his commands; by honoring him not only with our lips, but with all our heart and mind. And he says in Isaiah as well, "This people honors me with their lips but their heart is far from me."

4 Let us not merely call him Lord, for that will not save us. 2For he says, "Not everyone who says to me, Lord, Lord, will be saved, but he who does what is right." 3Thus, brothers, let us acknowledge him by our actions, by loving one another, by refraining from adultery, backbiting, and jealousy, and by being self-controlled, compassionate, kind. We ought to have sympathy for one another and not to be avaricious. Let us acknowledge him by acting in this way and not by doing the opposite. 4We ought not to have greater fear of men than of God. 5That is why, if you act in this way, the Lord said, "If you are gathered with me in my bosom and do not keep my commands, I will cast you out and will say to you: 'Depart from me. I do not know whence you come, you workers of iniquity.'"

5 Therefore, brothers, ceasing to tarry in this world, let us do the will of Him who called us, and let us not be afraid to leave this world. 2For the Lord said, "You will be like lambs among wolves." 3But Peter replied by saying, "What if the wolves tear the lambs to pieces?" 4Jesus said to Peter: "After their death the lambs should not fear the wolves, nor should you fear those who kill you and can do nothing more to you. But fear him who, when you are dead, has power over soul and body to cast them into the flames of hell." 5You must realize, brothers, that our stay in this world of the flesh is slight and short, but Christ's promise is great and wonderful, and means rest in the coming Kingdom and in eternal life. 6What, then, must we do to get these things, except to lead a holy and upright life and to regard these things of the world as alien to us and not to desire them? 7For in wanting to obtain these things we fall from the right way.

6 The Lord says, "No servant can serve two masters." If we want to serve both God and money, it will do us no good. 2"For what good does it do a man to gain the whole world and forfeit his life?" 3This world and the world to come are two enemies. 4This one means adultery, corruption, avarice, and deceit, while the other gives them up. 5We cannot, then, be friends of both. To get the one, we must give the other up. 6We think that it is better to hate what is here, for it is trifling, transitory, and perishable, and to value what is there—things good and imperishable. 7Yes, if we do the will of Christ, we shall find rest, but if not, nothing will save us from eternal punishment, if we fail to heed his commands. 8Furthermore, the Scripture also says in Ezekiel, "Though Noah and Job and Daniel should rise, they shall not save their children in captivity." ⁹If even such upright men as these cannot save their children by their uprightness, what assurance have we that we shall enter God's Kingdom if we fail to keep our baptism pure and undefiled? Or who will plead for us if we are not found to have holy and upright deeds?

7 So, my brothers, let us enter the contest, recognizing that it is at hand and that, while many come by sea to corruptible contests, not all win laurels, but only those who have struggled hard and competed well. ²Let us, then, compete so that we may all be crowned. ³Let us run the straight race, the incorruptible contest; and let many of us sail to it and enter it, so that we too may be crowned. And if we cannot all be crowned, let us at least come close to it. ⁴We must realize that if a contestant in a corruptible contest is caught cheating, he is flogged, removed, and driven from the course. ⁵What do you think? What shall be done with the man who cheats in the contest for the incorruptible? ⁶For in reference to those who have not guarded the seal, it says, "Their worm shall not die and their fire shall not be quenched, and they shall be a spectacle to all flesh."

8 So while we are on earth, let us repent. For we are like clay in a workman's hands. ²If a potter makes a vessel and it gets out of shape or breaks in his hands, he molds it over again; but if he has once thrown it into the flames of the furnace, he can do nothing more with it. Similarly, while we are in this world, let us too repent with our whole heart of the evil we have done in the flesh, so that we may be saved by the Lord while we have a chance to

repent. ³For once we have departed this world we can no longer confess there or repent any more. ⁴Thus, brothers, by doing the Father's will and by keeping the flesh pure and by abiding by the Lord's commands, we shall obtain eternal life. ⁵For the Lord says in the Gospel: "If you fail to guard what is small, who will give you what is great? For I tell you that he who is faithful in a very little, is faithful also in much. "This, then, is what he means: keep the flesh pure and the seal undefiled, so that we may obtain eternal life.

9 Moreover, let none of you say that this flesh will not be judged or rise again. ²Consider this: In what state were you saved? In what state did you regain your sight, if it was not while you were in this flesh? ³Therefore we should guard the flesh as God's temple. ⁴For just as you were called in the flesh, you will come in the flesh. ⁵If Christ the Lord who saved us was made flesh though he was at first spirit, and called us in this way, in the same way we too in this very flesh will receive our reward. ⁶Let us, then, love one another, so that we may all come to God's Kingdom. ⁷While we have an opportunity to be healed, let us give ourselves over to God, the physician, and pay him in return. ⁸How? By repenting with a sincere heart. ⁹For he foreknows everything, and realizes what is in our hearts. ¹⁰Let us then praise him, not with the mouth only, but from the heart, so that he may accept us as sons. ¹¹For the Lord said, "My brothers are those who do the will of my Father."

10 So, my brothers, let us do the will of the Father who called us, so that we may have life; and let our preference be the pursuit of virtue. Let us give up vice as the forerunner of our sins, and let us flee impiety, lest evils overtake us. [2]For if we are eager to do good, peace will pursue us. [3]This is the reason men cannot find peace. They give way to human fears, and prefer the pleasures of the present to the promises of the future. [4]For they do not realize what great torment the pleasures of the present bring, and what delight attaches to the promises of the future. [5]If they did these things by themselves, it might be tolerable. But they persist in teaching evil to innocent souls, and do not realize that they and their followers will have their sentence doubled.

11 Let us therefore serve God with a pure heart and we shall be upright. But if, by not believing in God's promises, we do not serve him, we shall be wretched. [2]For the word of the prophet says, "Wretched are the double-minded, those who doubt in their soul and say, 'We have heard these things long ago, even in our fathers' times, and day after day we have waited and have seen none of them.' [3]You fools! Compare yourselves to a tree. Take a vine: first it sheds its leaves, then comes a bud, and after this a sour grape, then a ripe bunch. [4]So my people too has had turmoils and troubles; but after that it will receive good things." [5]So, my brothers, we must not be double-minded. Rather must we patiently hold out in hope so that we may also gain our reward. [6]For "he can be trusted who promised" to pay each one the wages due for his work. [7]If, then, we have done what is right in God's eyes, we shall enter his Kingdom and receive the promises "which ear has not heard or eye seen, or which man's heart has not entertained."

12 Loving and doing what is right, we must be on the watch for God's Kingdom hour by hour, since we do not know the day when God will appear. ²For when someone asked the Lord when his Kingdom was going to come, he said, "When the two shall be one, and the outside like the inside, and the male with the female, neither male nor female." ³Now "the two" are "one" when we tell each other the truth and two bodies harbor a single mind with no deception. ⁴"The outside like the inside" means this: the inside" means the soul and "the outside" means the body. Just as your body is visible, so make your soul evident by your good deeds. ⁵Furthermore "the male with the female, neither male nor female," means this: that when a brother sees a sister he should not think of her sex, any more than she should think of his. ⁶When you do these things, he says, my Father's Kingdom will come.

13 Right now, my brothers, we must repent, and be alert for the good, for we are full of much stupidity and wickedness. We must wipe off from us our former sins and by heartfelt repentance be saved. And we must not seek to please men or desire to please only ourselves, but by doing what is right to please even outsiders, so that the Name may not be scoffed at on our account. ²For the Lord says, "My name is continually scoffed at by all peoples"; and again, "Alas for him through whom my name is scoffed at!" How is it scoffed at? By your failing to do what I want. ³For when the heathen hear God's oracles on our lips they marvel at their beauty and greatness. But afterwards, when they mark that our deeds are unworthy of the words we utter, they turn from this to scoffing, and say that it is a myth and a delusion. ⁴When, for instance, they hear from us that God says, "It is no credit to you if you love those who love you, but it is to your credit if you love your enemies and those who hate you," when they hear these things, they are amazed at such surpassing goodness. But when they see that we fail to love not only those who hate us, but even those who love us, then they mock at us and scoff at the Name.

14 So, my brothers, by doing the will of God our Father we shall belong to the first Church, the spiritual one, which was created before the sun and the moon. But if we fail to do the Lord's will, that passage of Scripture will apply to us which says, "My house has become a robber's den." So, then, we must choose to belong to the Church of life in order to be saved. ²I do not suppose that you are ignorant that the living "Church is the body of Christ. For Scripture says, "God made man male and female." The male is Christ; the female is the Church. The Bible, moreover, and the Apostles say that the Church is not limited to the present, but existed from the beginning. For it was spiritual, as was our Jesus, and was made manifest in the last days to save us. ³Indeed, the Church which is spiritual was made manifest in the flesh of Christ, and so indicates to us that if any of us guard it in the flesh and do not corrupt it, he will get it in return by the Holy

Spirit. For this flesh is the antitype of the spirit. Consequently, no one who has corrupted the antitype will share in the reality. This, then, is what it means, brothers: Guard the flesh so that you may share in the spirit. 4Now, if we say that the Church is the flesh and the Christ is the spirit, then he who does violence to the flesh, does violence to the Church. Such a person, then, will not share in the spirit, which is Christ. 5This flesh is able to share in so great a life and immortality, because the Holy Spirit cleaves to it. Nor can one express or tell "what things the Lord has prepared" for his chosen ones.

15 The advice I have given about continence is not, I think, unimportant; and if a man acts on it, he will not regret it, but will save himself as well as me who advised him. For no small reward attaches to converting an errant and perishing soul, so that it may be saved. 2For this is how we can pay back God who created us, if the one who speaks and the one who hears do so with faith and love. 3Consequently, we must remain true to our faith and be upright and holy, so that we may petition God in confidence, who says, "Even while you are speaking, I will say, 'See, here I am.' 4Surely this saying betokens a great promise; for the Lord says of himself that he is more ready to give than we to ask. 5Let us, then, take our share of such great kindness and not begrudge ourselves the obtaining of such great blessings. For these sayings hold as much pleasure in store for those who act on them, as they do condemnation for those who disregard them.

16 So, brothers, since we have been given no small opportunity to repent, let us take the occasion to turn to God who has called us, while we still have One to accept us. 2For if we renounce these pleasures and master our souls by avoiding their evil lusts, we shall share in Jesus' mercy. 3Understand that "the day" of judgment is already "on its way like a furnace ablaze, and "the powers of heaven will dissolve"'" and the whole earth will be like lead melting in fire. Then men's secret and overt actions will be made clear. 4Charity, then, like repentance from sin, is a good thing. But fasting is better than prayer, and charity than both. "Love covers a multitude of sins," and prayer, arising from a good conscience, "rescues from death." Blessed is everyone who abounds in these things, for charity lightens sin.

17 Let us, then, repent with our whole heart, so that none of us will be lost. For if we have been commanded to do this too—to draw men away from idols and instruct them—how much more is it wrong for the soul which already knows God to perish? 2Consequently we must help one another and bring back those weak in goodness, so that we may all be saved; and convert and admonish one another. 3Not only at this moment, while the presbyters are preaching to us, should we appear believing and attentive. But when we have gone home, we should bear in mind the Lord's commands and not be diverted by worldly passions. Rather should we strive to come here more often and advance in the Lord's commands, so that "with a common mind" we may all be gathered together to gain life. 4For the Lord said, "I am coming to gather together all peoples, clans, and tongues." This refers to the day of his appearing, when he will come to redeem us, each according to his deeds. ⁵And "unbelievers will see his glory" and power, and they will be surprised to see the sovereignty of the world given to Jesus, and they will say, "Alas for us, for you really existed, and we neither recognized it nor believed, and we did not obey the presbyters who preached to us our salvation." And "their worm will not die and their fire will not be quenched, and they will be a spectacle to all flesh. ⁶He refers to that day of judgment when men will see those who were ungodly among us and who perverted the commands of Jesus Christ. ⁷But the upright who have done good and patiently endured tortures and hated the pleasures of the soul, when they see those who have done amiss and denied Jesus in word and act being punished with dreadful torments and undying fire, will give "glory to their God" and say, "There is hope for him who has served God with his whole heart."

18 Consequently we too must be of the number of those who give thanks and have served God, and not of the ungodly who are sentenced. ²For myself, I too am a grave sinner, and have not yet escaped temptation. I am still surrounded by the devil's devices, though I am anxious to pursue righteousness. My aim is to manage at least to approach it, for I am afraid of the judgment to come.

19 So, my brothers and sisters, after God's truth I am reading you an exhortation to heed what was there written, so that you may save yourselves and your reader. For compensation I beg you to repent with all your heart, granting yourselves salvation and life. By doing this we will set a goal for all the young who want to be active in the cause of religion and of God's goodness. 2We should not, moreover, be so stupid as to be displeased and vexed when anyone admonishes us and converts us from wickedness to righteousness. There are times when we do wrong unconsciously because of the double-mindedness and unbelief in our hearts, and "our understanding is darkened" by empty desires. 3Let us, then, do what is right so that we may finally be saved. Blessed are they who observe these injunctions; though they suffer briefly in this world, they will gather the immortal fruit of the resurrection. 4A religious man must not be downcast if he is miserable in the present. A time of blessedness awaits him. He will live again in heaven with his forefathers, and will rejoice in an eternity that knows no sorrow.

20 But you must not be troubled in mind by the fact that we see the wicked in affluence while God's slaves are in straitened circumstances. 2Brothers and sisters, we must have faith. We are engaged in the contest of the living God and are being trained by the present life in order to win laurels in the life to come. 3None of the upright has obtained his reward quickly, but he waits for it. 4For were God to give the righteous their reward at once, our training would straightway be in commerce and not in piety, since we would give an appearance of uprightness, when pursuing, not religion, but gain. That is why the divine judgment punishes a spirit which is not upright, and loads it with chains. 5"To the only invisible God," the Father of truth, who dispatched to us the Savior and prince of immortality, through whom he also disclosed to us the truth and the heavenly life—to him be glory forever and ever. Amen.

The Letter of Ignatius, Bishop of Antioch to the Ephesians

∾

WRITTEN FROM SMYRNA, *where Ignatius and his military guard made a halt on their way to Rome via the northern road to Troas, this is the longest of his letters. Four delegates, including the modest and retiring bishop Onesimus, had been sent by the neighboring Ephesian church to greet and encourage the martyr. One of them, the deacon Burrhus, later accompanied Ignatius as far as Troas, and perhaps acted as his amanuensis (Philad. 11:2).*

Ignatius takes the occasion to thank the Ephesians for their kindness. While praising them for their unity and orthodoxy, he proceeds to warn them against schism and the prevalent Docetic heresy which was being disseminated by itinerant teachers.

THE TEXT

Heartiest greetings of pure joy in Jesus Christ from Ignatius, the "God-inspired," to the church at Ephesus in Asia. Out of the fullness of God the Father you have been blessed with large numbers and are predestined from eternity to enjoy forever continual and unfading glory. The source of your unity and election is genuine suffering which you undergo by the will of the Father and of Jesus Christ, our God. Hence you deserve to be considered happy.

1 I gave a godly welcome to your church which has so endeared itself to us by reason of your upright nature, marked as it is by faith in Jesus Christ, our Savior, and by love of him. You are imitators of God; and it was God's blood that stirred you up once more to do the sort of thing you do naturally and have now done to perfection. [2]For you were all zeal to visit me when you heard that I was being shipped as a prisoner from Syria for the sake of our common Name and hope. I hope, indeed, by your prayers to have the good fortune to fight with wild beasts in Rome, so that by doing this I can be a real disciple. [3]In God's name, therefore, I received your large congregation in the person of Onesimus, your bishop in this world, a man whose love is beyond words. My prayer is that you should love him in the spirit of Jesus Christ and all be like him. Blessed is He who let you have such a bishop. You deserved it.

2 Now about my fellow slave Burrhus, your godly deacon, who has been richly blessed. I very much want him to stay with me. He will thus bring honor on you and the bishop. Crocus too, who is a credit both to God and to you, and whom I received as a model of your love, altogether raised my spirits (May the Father of Jesus Christ grant him a similar comfort!), as did Onesimus, Bunthus, Euplus, and Fronto. In them I saw and loved you all. 2May I always be glad about you, that is, if I deserve to be! It is right, then, for you to render all glory to Jesus Christ, seeing he has glorified you. Thus, united in your submission, and subject to the bishop and the presbytery, you will be real saints.

3 I do not give you orders as if I were somebody important. For even if I am a prisoner for the Name, I have not yet reached Christian perfection. I am only beginning to be a disciple, so I address you as my fellow students. I needed your coaching in faith, encouragement, endurance, and patience. 2But since love forbids me to keep silent about you, I hasten to urge you to harmonize your actions with God's mind. For Jesus Christ—that life from which we can't be torn—is the Father's mind, as the bishops too, appointed the world over, reflect the mind of Jesus Christ.

4 Hence you should act in accord with the bishop's mind, as you surely do. Your presbytery, indeed, which deserves its name and is a credit to God, is as closely tied to the bishop as the strings to a harp. Wherefore your accord and harmonious love is a hymn to Jesus Christ. 2Yes, one and all, you should form yourselves into a choir, so that, in perfect harmony and taking your pitch from God, you may sing in unison and with one voice to the Father through Jesus Christ. Thus he will heed you, and by

your good deeds he will recognize you are members of his Son. Therefore you need to abide in irreproachable unity if you really want to be God's members forever.

5 If in so short a time I could get so close to your bishop—I do not mean in a natural way, but hi a spiritual—how much more do I congratulate you on having such intimacy with him as the Church enjoys with Jesus Christ, and Jesus Christ with the Father. That is how unity and harmony come to prevail everywhere. 2Make no mistake about it. If anyone is not inside the sanctuary, he lacks God's bread. And if the prayer of one or two has great avail, how much more that of the bishop and the total Church. 3He who fails to join in your worship shows his arrogance by the very fact of becoming a schismatic. It is written, moreover, "God resists the proud." Let us, then, heartily avoid resisting the bishop so that we may be subject to God.

6 The more anyone sees the bishop modestly silent, the more he should revere him. For everyone the Master of the house sends on his business, we ought to receive as the One who sent him. It is clear, then, that we should regard the bishop as the Lord himself. 2Indeed, Onesimus spoke very highly of your godly conduct, that you were all living by the truth and harboring no sectarianism. Nay, you heed nobody beyond what he has to say truthfully about Jesus Christ.

7 Some, indeed, have a wicked and deceitful habit of flaunting the Name about, while acting in a way unworthy of God. You must avoid them like wild beasts. For they are mad dogs which bite on the sly. You must be on your guard against them for it is hard to heal their bite. ²There is only one physician—of flesh yet spiritual, born yet unbegotten, God incarnate, genuine life in the midst of death, sprung from Mary as well as God, first subject to suffering then beyond it—Jesus Christ our Lord.

8 Let no one mislead you, as, indeed, you are not misled, being wholly God's. For when you harbor no dissension that can harass you, then you are indeed living in God's way. A cheap sacrifice I am, but I dedicate myself to you Ephesians—a church forever famous. ²Carnal people cannot act spiritually, or spiritual people carnally, just as faith cannot act like unbelief, or unbelief like faith. But even what you do in the flesh you do spiritually. For you do everything under Christ's control.

9 I have heard that some strangers came your way with a wicked teaching. But you did not let them sow it among you. You stopped up your ears to prevent admitting what they disseminated. Like stones of God's Temple, ready for a building of God the Father, you are being hoisted up by Jesus Christ, as with a crane (that's the cross!), while the rope you use is the Holy Spirit. Your faith is what lifts you up, while love is the way you ascend to God.

²You are all taking part in a religious procession, carrying along with you your God, shrine, Christ, and your holy objects, and decked out from tip to toe in the commandments of Jesus Christ. I too am enjoying it all, because I can talk with you in a letter, and congratulate you on changing your old way of life and setting your love on God alone.

10 "Keep on praying" for others too, for there is a chance of their being converted and getting to God. Let them, then, learn from you at least by your actions. ²Return their bad temper with gentleness; their boasts with humility; their abuse with prayer. In the face of their error, be "steadfast in the faith." Return their violence with mildness and do not be intent on getting your own back. ³By our patience let us show we are their brothers, intent on imitating the Lord, seeing which of us can be the more wronged, robbed, and despised. Thus no devil's weed will be found among you; but thoroughly pure and self-controlled, you will remain body and soul united to Jesus Christ.

11 The last days are here. So let us abase ourselves and stand in awe of God's patience, lest it turn out to be our condemnation. Either let us fear the wrath to come or let us value the grace we have: one or the other. Only let our lot be genuine life in Jesus Christ. ²Do not let anything catch your eye besides him, for whom I carry around these chains—my spiritual pearls! Through them I want to rise from the dead by your prayers. May I ever share in these, so that I may be numbered among the Ephesian Christians who, by the might of Jesus Christ, have always been of one mind with the very apostles.

12 I realize who I am and to whom I am writing. I am a convict; you have been freed. I am in danger; you are safe. ²You are the route for God's victims. You have been initiated into the [Christian] mysteries with Paul, a real saint and martyr, who deserves to be congratulated. When I come to meet God may I follow in his footsteps, who in all his letters mentions your union with Christ Jesus.

13 Try to gather together more frequently to celebrate God's Eucharist and to praise him. For when you meet with frequency, Satan's powers are overthrown and his destructiveness is undone by the unanimity of your faith. 2There is nothing better than peace, by which all strife in heaven and earth is done away.

14 You will not overlook any of this if you have a thorough belief in Jesus Christ and love him. That is the beginning and end of life: faith the beginning and love the end. And when the two are united you have God, and everything else that has to do with real goodness is dependent on them. 2No one who professes faith falls into sin, nor does one who has learned to love, hate. "The tree is known by its fruit." Similarly, those who profess to be Christ's will be recognized by their actions. For what matters is not a momentary act of professing, but being persistently motivated by faith.

15 It is better to keep quiet and be real, than to chatter and be unreal. It is a good thing to teach if, that is, the teacher practices what he preaches. There was one such Teacher, who "spoke and it was done; and what he did in silence is worthy of the Father." 2He who has really grasped what Jesus said can appreciate his silence. Thus he will be perfect: his words will mean action, and his very silence will reveal his character.

3The Lord overlooks nothing. Even secrets are open to him. Let us, then, do everything as if he were dwelling in us. Thus we shall be his temples and he will be within us as our God—as he actually is. This will be clear to us just to the extent that we love him rightly.

16 Make no mistake, my brothers: adulterers will not inherit God's Kingdom. If, then, those who act carnally suffer death, how much more shall those who by wicked teaching corrupt God's faith for which Jesus Christ was crucified. Such a vile creature will go to the unquenchable fire along with anyone who listens to him.

17 The reason the Lord let the ointment be poured on his head was that he might pass on the aroma of incorruption to the Church. Do not be anointed with the foul smell of the teaching of the prince of this world, lest he capture you and rob you of the life ahead of you. ²Why do we not all come to our senses by accepting God's knowledge, which is Jesus Christ? Why do we stupidly perish, ignoring the gift which the Lord has really sent?

18 I am giving my life (not that it's worth much!) for the cross, which unbelievers find a stumbling block, but which means to us salvation and eternal life. "Where is the wise man? Where is the debater?" Where are the boasts of those supposedly intelligent? ²For our God, Jesus the Christ, was conceived by Mary, in God's plan being sprung both from the seed of David and from the Holy Spirit. He was born and baptized that by his Passion he might hallow water.

19 Now, Mary's virginity and her giving birth escaped the notice of the prince of this world, as did the Lord's death—those three secrets crying to be told, but wrought in God's silence: [2]How, then, were they revealed to the ages? A star shone in heaven brighter than all the stars. Its light was indescribable and its novelty caused amazement. The rest of the stars, along with the sun and the moon, formed a ring around it; yet it outshone them all, and there was bewilderment whence this unique novelty had arisen. [3]As a result all magic lost its power and all witchcraft ceased. Ignorance was done away with, and the ancient kingdom [of evil] was utterly destroyed, for God was revealing himself as a man, to bring newness of eternal life. What God had prepared was now beginning. Hence everything was in confusion as the destruction of death was being taken in hand.

20 If Jesus Christ allows me, in answer to your prayers, and it is his will, I will explain to you more about [God's] plan in a second letter I intend to write. I have only touched on this plan in reference to the New Man Jesus Christ, and how it involves believing in him and loving him, and entails his Passion and resurrection. [2]I will do this especially if the Lord shows me that you are all, every one of you, meeting together under the influence of the grace that we owe to the Name, in one faith and in union with Christ, who was "descended from David according to the flesh" and is Son of man and Son of God. At these meetings you should heed the bishop and presbytery attentively, and break one loaf, which is the medicine of immortality, and the antidote which wards off death but yields continuous life in union with Jesus Christ.

21 I am giving my life for you and for those whom you, to God's honor, sent to Smyrna. I am writing to you from there, giving the Lord thanks and embracing Polycarp and you too in my love. Bear me in mind, as Jesus Christ does you. [2]Pray for the church in Syria, whence I am being sent off to Rome as a prisoner. I am the least of the faithful there—yet I have been privileged to serve God's honor. Farewell in God the Father and in Jesus Christ, our common hope.

The Letter of Ignatius,
Bishop of Antioch
to the Magnesians

∞

LIKE THE EPHESIANS, the Christians at Magnesia (a town some fifteen miles from Ephesus) sent delegates to greet Ignatius in Smyrna. Among them was their youthful bishop, Damas. In his letter to them Ignatius instructs them on not presuming on the youthfulness of their bishop, emphasizes the importance of unity and subjection to the Church officers, and warns them against Judaistic errors.

THE TEXT

Every good wish in God the Father and in Jesus Christ from Ignatius, the "God-inspired," to the church at Magnesia on the Maeander. In Christ Jesus, our Savior, I greet your church which, by reason of its union with him, is blessed with the favor of God the Father.

1 I was delighted to hear of your well-disciplined and godly love; and hence, impelled by faith in Jesus Christ, I decided to write to you. ²Privileged as I am to have this distinguished and godly name, I sing the praises of the churches, even while I am a prisoner. I want them to confess that Jesus Christ, our perpetual Life, united flesh with spirit. I want them, too, to unite their faith with love—there is nothing better than that. Above all, I want them to confess the union of Jesus with the Father. If, with him to support us, we put up with all the spite of the prince of this world and manage to escape, we shall get to God.

2 Yes, I had the good fortune to see you, in the persons of Damas your bishop (he's a credit to God!), and of your worthy presbyters, Bassus and Apollonius, and of my fellow slave, the deacon Zotion. I am delighted with him, because he submits to the bishop as to God's grace, and to the presbytery as to the law of Jesus Christ.

3 Now, it is not right to presume on the youthfulness of your bishop. You ought to respect him as fully as you respect the authority of God the Father. Your holy presbyters, I know, have not taken unfair advantage of his apparent youthfulness, but in their godly wisdom have deferred to him—nay, rather, not so much to him as to the Father of Jesus Christ, who is everybody's bishop. ²For the honor, then, of him who loved us, we ought to obey without any dissembling, since the real issue is not that a man misleads a bishop whom he can see, but that he defrauds the One who is invisible. In such a case he must reckon, not with a human being, but with God who knows his secrets.

4 We have not only to be called Christians, but to be Christians. It is the same thing as calling a man a bishop and then doing everything in disregard of him. Such people seem to me to be acting against their conscience, since they do not come to the valid and authorized services.

5 Yes, everything is coming to an end, and we stand before this choice—death or life—and everyone will go "to his own place." One might say similarly, there are two coinages, one God's, the other the world's. Each bears its own stamp—unbelievers that of this world; believers, who are spurred by love, the stamp of God the Father through Jesus Christ. And if we do not willingly die in union with his Passion, we do not have his life in us.

6 I believed, then, that I saw your whole congregation in these people I have mentioned, and I loved you all. Hence I urge you to aim to do everything in godly agreement. Let the bishop preside in God's place, and the presbyters take the place of the apostolic council, and let the deacons (my special favorites) be entrusted with the ministry of Jesus Christ who was with the Father from eternity and appeared at the end [of the world]. ²Taking, then, the same attitude as God, you should all respect one another. Let no one think of his neighbor in a carnal way; but always love one another in the spirit of Jesus Christ. Do not let there be anything to divide you, but be in accord with the bishop and your leaders. Thus you will be an example and a lesson of incorruptibility.

7 As, then, the Lord did nothing without the Father (either on his own or by the apostles) because he was at one with him, so you must not do anything without the bishop and presbyters. Do not, moreover, try to convince yourselves that anything done on your own is commendable. Only what you do together is right. Hence you must have one prayer, one petition, one mind, one hope, dominated by love and unsullied joy—that means you must have Jesus Christ. You cannot have anything better than that. ²Run off—all of you—to one temple of God, as it were, to one altar, to one Jesus Christ, who came forth from one Father, while still remaining one with him, and returned to him.

8 Do not be led astray by wrong views or by outmoded tales that count for nothing. For if we still go on observing Judaism, we admit we never received grace. ²The divine prophets themselves lived Christ Jesus' way. That is why they were persecuted, for they were inspired by his grace to convince unbelievers that God is one, and that he has revealed himself in his Son Jesus Christ, who is his Word issuing from the silence and who won the complete approval of him who sent him.

9 Those, then, who lived by ancient practices arrived at a new hope. They ceased to keep the Sabbath and lived by the Lord's Day, on which our life as well as theirs shone forth, thanks to Him and his death, though some deny this. Through this mystery we got our faith, and because of it we stand our ground so as to become disciples of Jesus Christ, our sole teacher. ²How, then, can we live without him when even the prophets, who were his disciples by the Spirit, awaited him as their teacher? He, then, whom they were rightly expecting, raised them from the dead, when he came.

10 We must not, then, be impervious to his kindness. Indeed, were he to act as we do, we should at once be done for. Hence, now we are his disciples, we must learn to live like Christians—to be sure, whoever bears any other name does not belong to God. ²Get rid, then, of the bad yeast—it has grown stale and sour—and be changed into new yeast, that is, into Jesus Christ. Be salted in him, so that none of you go bad, for your smell will give you away. ³It is monstrous to talk Jesus Christ and to live like a Jew. For Christianity did not believe in Judaism, but Judaism in Christianity. People of every tongue have come to believe in it, and so been united together in God.

11 I do not write in this way, my dear friends, because I have heard that any of you are like that. Rather do I, well aware of my humble position, want to caution you ahead, lest you fall a prey to stupid ideas, and to urge you to be thoroughly convinced of the birth, Passion, and resurrection, which occurred while Pontius Pilate was governor. Yes, all that was actually and assuredly done by Jesus Christ, our Hope. God forbid that any of you should lose it!

12 I want to be glad about you ever so much, if, that is, I deserve to be. For though I am a prisoner, I cannot compare with one of you who are free. I realize that you are not conceited, for you have Jesus Christ within you. And more, I know you are self-conscious when I praise you, just as Scripture says, "The upright man is his own accuser."

13 Make a real effort, then, to stand firmly by the orders of the Lord and the apostles, so that "whatever you do, you may succeed" in body and soul, in faith and love, in Son, Father, and Spirit, from first to last, along with your most distinguished bishop, your presbytery (that neatly plaited spiritual wreath!), and your godly deacons. ²Defer to the bishop and to one another as Jesus Christ did to the Father in the days of his flesh, and as the apostles did to Christ, to the Father, and to the Spirit. In that way we shall achieve complete unity.

14 I realize you are full of God. Hence I have counseled you but briefly. Remember me in your prayers, that I may get to God. Remember too the church in Syria—I do not deserve to be called a member of it. To be sure, I need your united and holy prayers and your love, so that the church in Syria may have the privilege of being refreshed by means of your church.

15 The Ephesians greet you from Smyrna. I am writing to you from there. Like you, they came here for God's glory and have revived me considerably, as has Polycarp, the bishop of Smyrna. The other churches also send their greetings to you in honor of Jesus Christ. Farewell—be at one with God, for you possess an unbreakable spirit, which is what Jesus Christ had.

The Letter of Ignatius, Bishop of Antioch to the Trallians

∾

*THE CHRISTIANS AT TRALLES (a town some seventeen miles
east of Magnesia) had sent their bishop, Polybius, to greet
Ignatius in Smyrna. His letter in response is characteristic. Its
leading themes are unity and obedience to the Church offi-
cials—themes provoked by the spreading danger of the Docetic
heresy. It contains, too, several flashes that reveal Ignatius' character. Particularly striking is ch. 4, where he discloses his own
impetuous and fervent nature which contrasts with the calm
gentleness of Polybius.*

THE TEXT

Full hearty greetings in apostolic style, and every good wish from
Ignatius, the "God-inspired," to the holy church at Tralles in
Asia. You are dear to God, the Father of Jesus Christ, elect and a

real credit to him, being completely at peace by reason of the Passion of Jesus Christ, who is our Hope, since we shall rise in union with him.

1 Well do I realize what a character you have—above reproach and steady under strain. It is not just affected, but it comes naturally to you, as I gathered from Polybius, your bishop. By God's will and that of Jesus Christ, he came to me in Smyrna, and so heartily congratulated me on being a prisoner for Jesus Christ that in him I saw your whole congregation. ²I welcomed, then, your godly good will, which reached me by him, and I gave thanks that I found you, as I heard, to be following God.

2 For when you obey the bishop as if he were Jesus Christ, you are (as I see it) living not in a merely human fashion but in Jesus Christ's way, who for our sakes suffered death that you might believe in his death and so escape dying yourselves. ²It is essential, therefore, to act in no way without the bishop, just as you are doing. Rather submit even to the presbytery as to the apostles of Jesus Christ. He is our Hope, and if we live in union with him now, we shall gain eternal life. Those too who are deacons of Jesus Christ's "mysteries" must give complete satisfaction to everyone. For they do not serve mere food and drink, but minister to God's Church. They must therefore avoid leaving themselves open to criticism, as they would shun fire.

3 Correspondingly, everyone must show the deacons respect. They represent Jesus Christ, just as the bishop has the role of the Father, and the presbyters are like God's council and an apostolic band. You cannot have a church without these. ²I am sure that you agree with me in this. In your bishop I received the very model of your love, and I have him with me. His very bearing is a great lesson, while his gentleness is most forceful. I imagine even the godless respect him. ³While I could write about this matter more sharply, I spare you out of love. Since, too, I am a convict, I have not thought it my place to give you orders like an apostle.

4 God has granted me many an inspiration, but I keep my limits, lest boasting should be my undoing. For what I need most at this point is to be on my guard and not to heed flatterers. Those who tell me . . . they are my scourge. ²To be sure, I am ever so eager to be a martyr, but I do not know if I deserve to be. Many people have no notion of my impetuous ambition. Yet it is all the more a struggle for me. What I need is gentleness by which the prince of this world is overthrown.

5 Am I incapable of writing to you of heavenly things? No, indeed; but I am afraid to harm you, seeing you are mere babes. You must forgive me, but the chances are you could not accept what I have to say and would choke yourselves. ²Even in my own case, it is not because I am a prisoner and can grasp heavenly mysteries, the ranks of the angels, the array of principalities, things visible and invisible—it is not because of all that that I am a genuine disciple as yet. There is plenty missing, if we are not going to be forsaken by God.

6 I urge you, therefore—not I, but Jesus Christ's love—use only Christian food. Keep off foreign fare, by which I mean heresy. [2]For those people mingle Jesus Christ with their teachings just to gain your confidence under false pretenses. It is as if they were giving a deadly poison mixed with honey and wine, with the result that the unsuspecting victim gladly accepts it and drinks down death with fatal pleasure.

7 Be on your guard, then, against such people. This you will do by not being puffed up and by keeping very close to [our] God, Jesus Christ, and the bishop and the apostles' precepts. [2]Inside the sanctuary a man is pure; outside he is impure. That means: whoever does anything without bishop, presbytery, and deacons does not have a clear conscience.

8 It is not because I have heard of any such thing in your case that I write thus. No, in my love for you I am warning you ahead, since I foresee the devil's wiles. Recapture, then, your gentleness, and by faith (that's the Lord's flesh) and by love (that's Jesus Christ's blood) make yourselves new creatures. [2]Let none of you hold anything against his neighbor. Do not give the heathen opportunities whereby God's people should be scoffed at through the stupidity of a few. For, "Woe to him by whose folly my name is scoffed at before any."

9 Be deaf, then, to any talk that ignores Jesus Christ, of David's lineage, of Mary; who was really born, ate; and drank; was really persecuted under Pontius Pilate; was really crucified and died, in the sight of heaven and earth and the underworld. [2]He was really raised from the dead, for his Father raised him, just

as his Father will raise us, who believe on him, through Christ Jesus, apart from whom we have no genuine life.

10 And if, as some atheists (I mean unbelievers) say, his suffering was a sham (it's really they who are a sham!), why, then, am I a prisoner? Why do I want to fight with wild beasts? In that case I shall die to no purpose. Yes, and I am maligning the Lord too!

11 Flee, then, these wicked offshoots which produce deadly fruit. If a man taste of it, he dies outright. They are none of the Father's planting. ²For had they been, they would have shown themselves as branches of the cross, and borne immortal fruit. It is through the cross, by his suffering, that he summons you who are his members. A head cannot be born without limbs, since God stands for unity. It is his nature.

12 From Smyrna I send you my greetings in which the churches of God that are here with me join. They have altogether raised my spirits—yes, completely. ²My very chains which I carry around for Jesus Christ's sake, in my desire to get to God, exhort you, "Stay united and pray for one another!"

It is right that each one of you and especially the presbyters should encourage the bishop, in honor of the Father, Jesus Christ, and the apostles. ³Out of love I want you to heed me, so that my letter will not tell against you. Moreover, pray for me. By God's mercy I need your love if I am going to deserve the fate I long for, and not prove a "castaway."

13 The Smyrnaeans and Ephesians send their greetings with love. Remember the church of Syria in your prayers. I am not worthy to be a member of it: I am the least of their number. Farewell in Jesus Christ. Submit to the bishop as to [God's] law, and to the presbytery too. All of you, love one another with an undivided heart. ³My life is given for you, not only now but especially when I shall get to God. I am still in danger. But the Father is faithful: he will answer my prayer and yours because of Jesus Christ. Under his influence may you prove to be spotless.

The Letter of Ignatius, Bishop of Antioch to the Romans

∞

HIS FINAL LETTER from Smyrna, Ignatius writes to the church of Rome. Unlike his other letters, this one is not concerned with questions of heresy and Church unity. Rather is it an intensely personal document. In it he reveals most clearly the spirit of the Oriental martyr; and in a double way it is a letter to prepare his martyrdom. It is, on the one hand, a plea to the Romans not to interfere with the fate in store for him; and on the other hand it is, as it were, a letter to himself to brace him for the coming ordeal. It betrays an excess of zeal which is strange to most of us, and even repugnant to some. It must, however, be read in the light of the fact that Ignatius was tormented by the brutality of his Roman guard (his "ten leopards" as he calls them, ch. 5:1), and reacted with the intemperance of a man who had already given his life away. Some will find in the letter a perverted

*masochism; others will discern in it all the splendor of the mar-
tyr spirit. No one, however, will miss its burning sincerity or the
courageous zeal of a disciple to suffer with his Lord.*

*The significant place that the Roman church held in the
imagination of Ignatius is clear from the flattering inscription,
with its emphasis on the extensiveness of that church's charity,
and from the mention of Peter and Paul (in that order!) in ch. 4:3.*

THE TEXT

Greetings in Jesus Christ, the Son of the Father, from Ignatius,
the "God-inspired," to the church that is in charge of affairs in
Roman quarters and that the Most High Father and Jesus Christ,
his only Son, have magnificently embraced in mercy and love.
You have been granted light both by the will of Him who willed
all that is, and by virtue of your believing in Jesus Christ, our
God, and of loving him. You are a credit to God: you deserve your
renown and are to be congratulated. You deserve praise and success and are privileged to be without blemish. Yes, you rank first
in love, being true to Christ's law and stamped with the Father's
name. To you, then, sincerest greetings in Jesus Christ, our God,
for you cleave to his every commandment—observing not only
their letter but their spirit—being permanently filled with God's
grace and purged of every stain alien to it.

1 Since God has answered my prayer to see you godly people,
I have gone on to ask for more. I mean, it is as a prisoner for
Christ Jesus that I hope to greet you, if indeed it be [God's] will

that I should deserve to meet my end. Things are off to a good start. May I have the good fortune to meet my fate without interference! What I fear is your generosity which may prove detrimental to me. For you can easily do what you want to, whereas it is hard for me to get to God unless you let me alone. 2I do not want you to please men, but to please God, just as you are doing. For I shall never again have such a chance to get to God, nor can you, if you keep quiet, get credit for a finer deed. For if you quietly let me alone, people will see in me God's Word. But if you are enamored of my mere body, I shall, on the contrary, be a meaningless noise.

2 Grant me no more than to be a sacrifice for God while there is an altar at hand. Then you can form yourselves into a choir and sing praises to the Father in Jesus Christ that God gave the bishop of Syria the privilege of reaching the sun's setting when he summoned him from its rising. It is a grand thing for my life to set on the world, and for me to be on my way to God, so that I may rise in his presence.

3 You never grudged anyone. You taught others. So I want you to substantiate the lessons that you bid them heed. 2Just pray that I may have strength of soul and body so that I may not only talk [about martyrdom], but really want it. It is not that I want merely to be called a Christian, but actually to be one. Yes, if I prove to be one, then I can have the name. Then, too, I shall be a convincing Christian only when the world sees me no more. 3Nothing you can see has real value. Our God Jesus Christ, indeed, has revealed himself more clearly by returning to the Father. The greatness of Christianity lies in its being hated by the world, not in its being convincing to it.

4 I am corresponding with all the churches and bidding them all realize that I am voluntarily dying for God—if, that is, you do not interfere. I plead with you, do not do me an unseasonable kindness. Let me be fodder for wild beasts—that is how I can get to God. I am God's wheat and I am being ground by the teeth of wild beasts to make a pure loaf for Christ. ²I would rather that you fawn on the beasts so that they may be my tomb and no scrap of my body be left. Thus, when I have fallen asleep, I shall be a burden to no one. Then I shall be a real disciple of Jesus Christ when the world sees my body no more. Pray Christ for me that by these means I may become God's sacrifice. ³I do not give you orders like Peter and Paul. They were apostles: I am a convict. They were at liberty: I am still a slave. But if I suffer, I shall be emancipated by Jesus Christ; and united to him, I shall rise to freedom. Even now as a prisoner, I am learning to forgo my own wishes.

5 All the way from Syria to Rome I am fighting with wild beasts, by land and sea, night and day, chained as I am to ten leopards (I mean to a detachment of soldiers), who only get worse the better you treat them. But by their injustices I am becoming a better disciple, "though not for that reason am I acquitted." ²What a thrill I shall have from the wild beasts that are ready for me! I hope they will make short work of me. I shall coax them on to eat me up at once and not to hold off, as sometimes happens, through fear. And if they are reluctant, I shall force them to it. [3]Forgive me—I know what is good for me. Now is the moment I am beginning to be a disciple. May nothing seen or unseen begrudge me making my way to Jesus Christ. Come fire, cross, battling with wild beasts, wrenching of bones, mangling of limbs, crushing of my whole body, cruel tortures of the devil—only let me get to Jesus Christ!

6 Not the wide bounds of earth nor the kingdoms of this world will avail me anything. "I would rather die" and get to Jesus Christ, than reign over the ends of the earth. That is whom I am looking for—the One who died for us. That is whom I want—the One who rose for us. [2]I am going through the pangs of being born. Sympathize with me, my brothers! Do not stand in the way of my coming to life—do not wish death on me. Do not give back to the world one who wants to be God's; do not trick him with material things. Let me get into the clear light and manhood will be mine. [3]Let me imitate the Passion of my God. If anyone has Him in him, let him appreciate what I am longing for, and sympathize with me, realizing what I am going through.

7 The prince of this world wants to kidnap me and pervert my godly purpose. None of you, then, who will be there, must abet him. Rather be on my side—that is, on God's. Do not talk Jesus Christ and set your heart on the world. [2]Harbor no envy. If, when I arrive, I make a different plea, pay no attention to me. Rather heed what I am now writing to you. For though alive, it is with a passion for death that I am writing to you. My Desire has been crucified and there burns in me no passion for material things. There is living water in me, which speaks and says inside me, "Come to the Father." ³I take no delight in corruptible food or in the dainties of this life. What I want is God's bread, which is the flesh of Christ, who came from David's line; and for drink I want his blood: an immortal love feast indeed!

8 I do not want to live any more on a human plane. And so it shall be, if you want it to. Want it to, so that you will be wanted! Despite the brevity of my letter, trust my request. -Yes, Jesus Christ will clarify it for you and make you see I am really in earnest. He is the guileless mouth by which the Father has spoken truthfully. ³Pray for me that I reach my goal. I have written prompted, not by human passion, but by God's will. If I suffer, it will be because you favored me. If I am rejected, it will be because you hated me.

9 Remember the church of Syria in your prayers. In my place they have God for their shepherd. Jesus Christ alone will look after them —he, and your love. ²I blush to be reckoned among them, for I do not deserve it, being the least of them and an afterthought. Yet by his mercy I shall be something, if, that is, I get to God. ³With my heart I greet you; and the churches which have welcomed me, not as a chance passer-by, but in the name of Jesus Christ, send their love. Indeed, even those that did not naturally lie on my route went ahead to prepare my welcome in the different towns.

10 I am sending this letter to you from Smyrna by those praiseworthy Ephesians. With me, along with many others, is Crocus—a person very dear to me. [2]I trust you have had word about those who went ahead of me from Syria to Rome for God's glory. Tell them I am nearly there. They are all a credit to God and to you; so you should give them every assistance. [3]I am writing this to you on the twenty-fourth of August. Farewell, and hold out to the end with the patience of Jesus Christ.

The Letter of Ignatius, Bishop of Antioch to the Philadelphians

∾

AFTER LEAVING SMYRNA, Ignatius and his guard pressed on to Troas, where they made a halt before crossing by sea to Neapolis. It was from Troas that Ignatius wrote his last three letters. While their themes are the familiar ones of Church unity and heresy, their special importance lies in the fact that they are directed to churches that Ignatius had actually visited. (Philadelphia lay on the route he took from Laodicea to Smyrna.) They, therefore, reflect the issues of false teaching in more detail. The letter to the Philadelphians indicates the nature of the Judaistic errors which had been touched upon in the letter to the Magnesians; while that to the Smyrnaeans enlarges on Docetism.

Two friends of Ignatius, the deacons Philo and Rheus Agathopus, seem to have joined him in Troas after a stay in Philadelphia. They brought news of the church there and of the fact that the dissident element had slighted them and also attacked the martyr (chs. 6:3; 11). To answer these charges and to unmask the errors of his opponents, Ignatius wrote his letter. An interesting feature of it is his account of an actual debate he had with the Judaizers (ch. 8:2).

THE TEXT

Greetings in the blood of Jesus Christ from Ignatius, the "God-inspired," to the church of God the Father and the Lord Jesus Christ, which is at Philadelphia in Asia—an object of the divine mercy and firmly knit in godly unity. Yours is a deep, abiding joy in the Passion of our Lord; and by his overflowing mercy you are thoroughly convinced of his resurrection. You are the very personification of eternal and perpetual joy. This is especially true if you are at one with the bishop, and with the presbyters and deacons, who are on his side and who have been appointed by the will of Jesus Christ. By his Holy Spirit and in accordance with his own will he validated their appointment.

1 I well realize that this bishop of yours does not owe his ministry to deacons who resisted the bishop. his own efforts or to men. Nor is it to flatter his vanity that he holds this office which serves the common good. Rather does he owe it to the love of God the Father and the Lord Jesus Christ. I have been struck by his charming manner. 2By being silent he can do more than those who chatter. For he is in tune with the commandments as a harp is with its strings. For this reason I bless his godly mind, recognizing its virtue and perfection, and the way he lives in altogether godly composure, free from fitfulness and anger.

2 Since you are children of the light of truth, flee from schism and false doctrine. Where the Shepherd is, there follow like sheep. ²For there are many specious wolves who, by means of wicked pleasures, capture those who run God's race. In the face of your unity, however, they will not have a chance.

3 Keep away from bad pasturage. Jesus Christ does not cultivate it since the Father did not plant it. Not that I found schism among you—rather had you been sifted. As many as are God's and Jesus Christ's, they are on the bishop's side; and as many as repent and enter the unity of the church, they shall be God's, and thus they shall live in Jesus Christ's way. ³Make no mistake, my brothers, if anyone joins a schismatic he will not inherit God's Kingdom. If anyone walks in the way of heresy, he is out of sympathy with the Passion.

4 Be careful, then, to observe a single Eucharist.'" For there is one flesh of our Lord, Jesus Christ, and one cup of his blood that makes us one, and one altar, just as there is one bishop along with the presbytery and the deacons, my fellow slaves. In that way whatever you do is in line with God's will.

5 My brothers, in my abounding love for you I am overjoyed to put you on your guard—though it is not I, but Jesus Christ. Being a prisoner for his cause makes me the more fearful that I am still far from being perfect." Yet your prayers to God will make me perfect so that I may gain that fate which I have mercifully been allotted, by taking refuge in the "Gospel," as in Jesus' flesh, and in the "Apostles," as in the presbytery of the Church. 2And the "Prophets," let us love them too, because they anticipated the gospel in their preaching and hoped for and awaited him, and were saved by believing on him. Thus they were in Jesus Christ's unity. Saints they were, and we should love and admire them, seeing that Jesus Christ vouched for them and they form a real part of the gospel of our common hope.

6 "Now, if anyone preaches Judaism to you, pay no attention to him. For it is better to hear about Christianity from one of the circumcision than Judaism from a Gentile. If both, moreover, fail to talk about Jesus Christ, they are to me tombstones and graves of the dead," on which only human names are inscribed. 2Flee, then, the wicked tricks and snares of the prince of this world, lest his suggestions wear you down, and you waver in your love. Rather, meet together, all of you, with a single heart. 3I thank my God that in my relations with you I have nothing to be ashamed of. No one can brag secretly or openly that I was the slightest burden to anyone. I trust, too, that none of those I talked to will need to take what I say as a criticism of them.

7 Some there may be who wanted in a human way to mislead me, but the Spirit is not misled, seeing it comes from God. For "it knows whence it comes and whither it goes, and exposes what is secret. When I was with you I cried out, raising my voice—it was God's voice"—"Pay heed to the bishop, the presbytery, and the deacons." 2Some, it is true, suspected that I spoke thus because I had been told in advance that some of you were schismatics. But I swear by Him for whose cause I am a prisoner, that from no human channels did I learn this. It was the Spirit that kept on preaching in these words: "Do nothing apart from the bishop; keep your bodies as if they were God's temple; value unity; flee schism; imitate Jesus Christ as he imitated his Father."

8 I, then, was doing all I could, as a man utterly devoted to unity. Where there is schism and bad feeling, God has no place. The Lord forgives all who repent—if, that is, their repentance brings them into God's unity and to the bishop's council. I put my confidence in the grace of Jesus Christ. He will release you from all your chains. ²I urge you, do not do things in cliques, but act as Christ's disciples. When I heard some people saying, "If I don't find it in the original documents, I don't believe it is the gospel," I answered them, "But it is written there." They retorted, "That's just the question. To my mind it is Jesus Christ who is the original documents. The inviolable archives are his cross and death and his resurrection and the faith that came by him. It is by these things and through your prayers that I want to be justified.

9 Priests are a fine thing, but better still is the High Priest who was entrusted with the Holy of Holies. He alone was entrusted with God's secrets. He is the door to the Father. Through it there enter Abraham, Isaac, and Jacob, the prophets and apostles and the Church. All these find their place in God's unity. ²But there is something special about the gospel—I mean the coming of the Savior, our Lord Jesus Christ, his Passion and resurrection. The beloved prophets announced his coming; but the gospel is the crowning achievement forever. All these things, taken together, have their value, provided you hold the faith in love.

10 Thanks to your prayers and to the love that you have for me in Christ Jesus, news has reached me that the church at Antioch in Syria is at peace. Consequently, it would be a nice thing for you, as a church of God, to elect a deacon to go there on a mission, as God's representative, and at a formal service to congratulate them and glorify the Name. [2]He who is privileged to perform such a ministry will enjoy the blessing of Jesus Christ, and you too will win glory. If you really want to do this for God's honor, it is not impossible, just as some of the churches in the vicinity have already sent bishops; others presbyters and deacons.

11 Now about Philo, the deacon from Cilicia. He is well spoken of and right now he is helping me in God's cause, along with Rheus Agathopus—a choice person—who followed me from Syria and so has said good-by to this present life. They speak well of you, and I thank God on your account that you welcomed them, as the Lord does you. I hope that those who slighted them will be redeemed by Jesus Christ's grace. [2]The brothers in Troas send their love and greetings. It is from there that I am sending this letter to you by Burrhus. The Ephesians and Smyrnaeans have done me the honor of sending him to be with me. They in turn will be honored by Jesus Christ, on whom they have set their hope with body, soul, spirit, faith, love, and a single mind. Farewell in Christ Jesus, our common Hope.

The Letter of Ignatius, Bishop of Antioch to the Smyrnaeans

∾

AT SMYRNA Ignatius had come into personal contact with Docetism. To his mind this presented such an imminent danger to the church there that his letter plunges at once into the theme with a vigorous affirmation of the reality of Christ's Passion and resurrection. Only toward the end of his letter does he refer to the hospitality he had received during his stay. The number of greetings at the conclusion indicate the warm welcome he had been given.

It is worthy of notice that he adopts a harsher attitude to the Docetic heretics than to the Judaizers. The former are to be avoided altogether—he will not even mention their names (chs. 4:1; 5:3; 7:2).

Another interesting feature of this letter is the first appearance in Christian literature of the phrase "the Catholic Church" (ch. 8:2). It stands for the universal and transcendent Church in contrast to the local congregation.

THE TEXT

Heartiest greetings in all sincerity and in God's Word from Ignatius, the "God-inspired," to the church of God the Father and the beloved Jesus Christ, which is at Smyrna in Asia. By God's mercy you have received every gift; you abound in faith and love, and are lacking in no gift. You are a wonderful credit to God and real saints.

1 I extol Jesus Christ, the God who has granted you such wisdom. For I detected that you were fitted out with an unshakable faith, being nailed, as it were, body and soul to the cross of the Lord Jesus Christ, and being rooted in love by the blood of Christ. Regarding our Lord, you are absolutely convinced that on the human side he was actually sprung from David's line, Son of God according to God's will and power, actually born of a virgin, baptized by John, that "all righteousness might be fulfilled by him," and actually crucified for us in the flesh, under Pontius Pilate and Herod the Tetrarch. (We are part of His fruit which grew out of his most blessed Passion.) And thus, by his resurrection, he raised a standard" to rally his saints and faithful forever—whether Jews or Gentiles—in one body of his Church.

2 For it was for our sakes that he suffered all this, to save us. And he genuinely suffered, as even he genuinely raised himself. It is not as some unbelievers say, that his Passion was a sham. It's

they who are a sham! Yes, and their fate will fit their fancies—
they will be ghosts and apparitions.

3 For myself, I am convinced and believe that even after the
resurrection he was in the flesh. [2]Indeed, when he came to Peter
and his friends, he said to them, "Take hold of me, touch me and
see that I am not a bodiless ghost." And they at once touched him
and were convinced, clutching his body and his very breath. For
this reason they despised death itself, and proved its victors.
Moreover, after the resurrection he ate and drank with them as a
real human being, although in spirit he was united with the
Father.

4 I urge these things on you, my friends, although I am well
aware that you agree with me. But I warn you in advance against
wild beasts in human shapes. You must not only refuse to receive
them, but if possible, you must avoid meeting them. Just pray for
them that they may somehow repent, hard as that is. Yet Jesus
Christ, our genuine life, has the power to bring it about. [2]If what
our Lord did is a sham, so is my being in chains. Why, then, have
I given myself up completely to death, fire, sword, and wild
beasts? For the simple reason that near the sword means near
God. To be with wild beasts means to be with God. But it must
all be in the name of Jesus Christ. To share in his Passion I go
through everything, for he who became the perfect man gives me
the strength.

5 Yet in their ignorance some deny him—or rather have been
denied by him, since they advocate death rather than the truth.

The prophets and the law of Moses have failed to convince them —nay, to this very day the gospel and the sufferings of each one of us have also failed, for they class our sufferings with Christ's. [2]What good does anyone do me by praising me and then reviling my Lord by refusing to acknowledge that he carried around live flesh? He who denies this has completely disavowed him and carries a corpse around. [3]The names of these people, seeing they are unbelievers, I am not going to write down. No, far be it from me even to recall them until they repent and acknowledge the Passion, which means our resurrection.

6 Let no one be misled: heavenly beings, the splendor of angels, and principalities, visible and invisible, if they fail to believe in Christ's blood, they too are doomed. "Let him accept it who can." Let no one's position swell his head, for faith and love are everything—there is nothing preferable to them. [2]Pay close attention to those who have wrong notions about the grace of Jesus Christ, which has come to us, and note how at variance they are with God's mind. They care nothing about love: they have no concern for widows or orphans, for the oppressed, for those in prison or released, for the hungry or the thirsty.

7 They hold aloof from the Eucharist and from services of prayer, because they refuse to admit that the Eucharist is the flesh of our Savior Jesus Christ, which suffered for our sins and which, in his goodness, the Father raised [from the dead]. Consequently those who wrangle and dispute God's gift face death. They would have done better to love and so share in the resurrection. 2The right thing to do, then, is to avoid such people and to talk about them neither in private nor in public. Rather pay attention to the prophets and above all to the gospel. There we get a clear picture of the Passion and see that the resurrection has really happened.

8 Flee from schism as the source of mischief. You should all follow the bishop as Jesus Christ did the Father. Follow, too, the presbytery as you would the apostles; and respect the deacons as you would God's law. Nobody must do anything that has to do with the Church without the bishop's approval. You should regard that Eucharist as valid which is celebrated either by the bishop or by someone he authorizes. 2Where the bishop is present, there let the congregation gather, just as where Jesus Christ is, there is the Catholic Church. Without the bishop's supervision, no baptisms or love feasts are permitted. On the other hand, whatever he approves pleases God as well. In that way everything you do will be on the safe side and valid.

9 It is well for us to come to our senses at last, while we still have a chance to repent and turn to God. It is a fine thing to acknowledge God and the bishop. He who pays the bishop honor has been honored by God. But he who acts without the bishop's knowledge is in the devil's service. 2By God's grace may you have an abundance of everything! You deserve it. You have brought me no end of comfort; may Jesus Christ do the same for you! Whether I was absent or present, you gave me your love. May God requite you! If for his sake you endure everything, you will get to him.

10 It was good of you to welcome Philo and Rheus Agathopus as deacons of the Christ God. They accompanied me in God's cause, and they thank the Lord on your behalf that you provided them every comfort. I can assure you you will lose nothing by it. ²Prisoner as I am, I am giving my life for you—not that it's worth much! You did not scorn my chains and were not ashamed of them. Neither will Jesus Christ be ashamed of you. You can trust him implicitly!

11 Your prayers have reached out as far as the church at Antioch in Syria. From there I have come, chained with these magnificent chains, and I send you all greetings. I do not, of course, deserve to be a member of that church, seeing I am the least among them. Yet it was [God's] will to give me the privilege—not, indeed, for anything I had done of my own accord, but by his grace. Oh, I want that grace to be given me in full measure, that by your prayers I may get to God! ²Well, then, so that your own conduct may be perfect on earth and in heaven, it is right that your church should honor God by sending a delegate in his name to go to Syria and to congratulate them on being at peace, on recovering their original numbers, and on having their own corporate life restored to them. ³To my mind that is what God would want you to do: to send one of your number with a letter, and thus join with them in extolling the calm which God has granted them, and the fact that they have already reached a haven, thanks to your prayers. Seeing you are perfect, your intentions must be perfect as well. Indeed, if you want to do what is right, God stands ready to give you his help.

12 The brothers in Troas send their love to you. From there I am sending this letter to you by Burrhus. You joined with your Ephesian brothers in sending him to be with me, and he has altogether raised my spirits. I wish everyone would be like him, since he is a model of what God's ministry should be. God's grace will repay him for all he has done for me. ²Greetings to your bishop (he is such a credit to God!), and to your splendid presbytery and to my fellow slaves the deacons, and to you all, every one of you, in Jesus Christ's name, in his flesh and blood, in his Passion and resurrection, both bodily and spiritual, and in unity—both God's and yours. Grace be yours, and mercy, peace, and endurance, forever.

13 Greetings to the families of my brothers, along with their wives and children, and to the virgins enrolled with the widows. I bid you farewell in the Father's power. Philo, who is with me, sends you greetings. ²Greetings to Tavia's family. I want her to be firmly and thoroughly grounded in faith and love. Greetings to Alce, who means a great deal to me, and to the inimitable Daphnus and to Eutecnus and to each one of you. Farewell in God's grace.

The Letter of Ignatius, Bishop of Antioch to Polycarp

∿

ALONG WITH THE LETTER *to the church of Smyrna, Ignatius wrote to its bishop, Polycarp. One of the most distinguished figures of the Early Church, who crowned his old age with martyrdom, Polycarp had given Ignatius a generous welcome which the latter mentions in other letters (Eph., ch. 21; Mag., ch. 15). This is an intimate and personal letter—the shortest of them all. Polycarp was the younger of the two men, perhaps in his early forties, and Ignatius is characteristically forthright in his advice. That the latter was most highly regarded by the bishop of Smyrna is clear from his own letter to the Philippians and from his making a collection of Ignatius' correspondence (Polycarp, Phil., ch. 13).*

The sense of Christian solidarity which bound together the local churches is evident from the various delegations which

Ignatius received in Smyrna. The suggestion, however, in the letter to the Philadelphians and repeated in this one to Polycarp, that the churches should send delegates as far as Syrian Antioch to congratulate the Christians on the cessation of persecution, is a telling witness to the universal consciousness of the local congregations. In a day when travel was neither easy nor free from danger, the dispatching of such messengers reflects the deep unity of the Christian brotherhood.

THE TEXT

Heartiest greetings from Ignatius, the "God-inspired," to Polycarp, who is bishop of the church at Smyrna—or rather who has God the Father and the Lord Jesus Christ for his bishop.

1 While I was impressed with your godly mind, which is fixed, as it were, on an immovable rock, I am more than grateful that I was granted the sight of your holy face. ²God grant I may never forget it! By the grace which you have put on, I urge you to press forward in your race and to urge everybody to be saved. Vindicate your position by giving your whole attention to its material and spiritual sides. Make unity your concern—there is nothing better than that. Lend everybody a hand, as the Lord does you. "Out of love be patient" with everyone, as indeed you are. ³Devote yourself to continual prayer. Ask for increasing insight. Be ever on the watch by keeping your spirit alert. Take a personal interest in those you talk to, just as God does. "Bear the diseases" of everyone like an athlete in perfect form. The greater the toil, the greater the gain.

2 It is no credit to you if you are fond of good pupils. Rather by your gentleness subdue those who are annoying. Not every wound is healed by the same plaster. Relieve spasms of pain with poultices. 2In all circumstances be "wise as a serpent," and perpetually "harmless as a dove." The reason you have a body as well as a soul is that you may win the favor of the visible world. But ask that you may have revelations of what is unseen. In that way you will lack nothing and have an abundance of every gift.

3Just as pilots demand winds and a storm-tossed sailor a harbor, so times like these demand a person like you. With your help we will get to God. As God's athlete, be sober. The prize, as you very well know, is immortality and eternal life. Bound as I am with chains that you kissed, I give my whole self for you cheap sacrifice though it is.

3 You must not be panic-stricken by those who have an air of credibility but who teach heresy. Stand your ground like an anvil under the hammer. A great athlete must suffer blows to conquer. And especially for God's sake must we put up with everything, so that he will put up with us. 2Show more enthusiasm than you do. Mark the times. Be on the alert for him who is above time, the Timeless, the Unseen, the One who became visible for our sakes, who was beyond touch and passion, yet who for our sakes became subject to suffering, and endured everything for us.

4 Widows must not be neglected. After the Lord you must be their protector. Do not let anything be done without your consent; and do not do anything without God's, as indeed you do not. Stand firm. ²Hold services more often. Seek out everybody by name. ³Do not treat slaves and slave girls contemptuously. Neither must they grow insolent. But for God's glory they must give more devoted service, so that they may obtain from God a better freedom. Moreover, they must not be overanxious to gain their freedom at the community's expense, lest they prove to be slaves of selfish passion.

5 Flee from such wicked practices—nay, rather, preach against them.

Tell my sisters to love the Lord and to be altogether contented with their husbands. Similarly urge my brothers in the name of Jesus Christ "to love their wives as the Lord loves the Church." ²If anyone can live in chastity for the honor of the Lord's flesh, let him do so without ever boasting. If he boasts of it, he is lost; and if he is more highly honored than the bishop, his chastity is as good as forfeited. It is right for men and women who marry to be united with the bishop's approval. In that way their marriage will follow God's will and not the promptings of lust. Let everything be done so as to advance God's honor.

6 Pay attention to the bishop so that God will pay attention to you. I give my life as a sacrifice (poor as it is) for those who are obedient to the bishop, the presbyters, and the deacons. Along with them may I get my share of God's reward! Share your hard training together—wrestle together, run together, suffer together, go to bed together, get up together, as God's stewards, assessors, and assistants. 2Give satisfaction to Him in whose ranks you serve and from whom you get your pay. Let none of you prove a deserter. Let your baptism be your arms; your faith, your helmet; your love, your spear; your endurance, your armor. Let your deeds be your deposits, so that you will eventually get back considerable savings. Be patient, then, and gentle with each other, as God is with you. May I always be happy about you!

7 News has reached me that, thanks to your prayers, the church at Antioch in Syria is now at peace. At this I have taken new courage and, relying on God, I have set my mind at rest—assuming, that is, I may get to God through suffering, and at the resurrection prove to be your disciple. 2So, my dear Polycarp (and how richly God has blessed you!), you ought to call a most religious council and appoint somebody whom you regard as especially dear and diligent, and who can act as God's messenger. You should give him the privilege of going to Syria and of advancing God's glory by extolling your untiring generosity. 3A Christian does not control his own life, but gives his whole time to God. This is God's work, and when you have completed it, it will be yours as well. For God's grace gives me confidence that you are ready to act generously when it comes to his business. It is because I am well aware of your earnest sincerity that I limit my appeal to so few words.

8 I have been unable to write to all the churches because I

am sailing at once (so God has willed it) from Troas to Neapolis. I want you, therefore, as one who has the mind of God, to write to the churches ahead and to bid them to do the same. Those who can should send representatives, while the others should send letters by your own delegates. In that way you will win renown, such as you deserve, by an act that will be remembered forever. [2]Greetings to every one of you personally, and to the widow of Epitropus with her children and her whole family. Greetings to my dear Attalus. Greetings to the one who is to be chosen to go to Syria. Grace will ever be with him and with Polycarp who sends him. I bid you farewell as always in our God, Jesus Christ. May you abide in him and so share in the divine unity and be under God's care. Greetings to Alce, who means a great deal to me. Farewell in the Lord.

The Letter of Saint Polycarp, Bishop of Smyrna, to the Philippians

∾

THE TEXT

POLYCARP AND THE PRESBYTERS with him, to the church of God that sojourns at Philippi; may mercy and peace be multiplied to you from God Almighty and Jesus Christ, our Savior.

1 I rejoice with you greatly in our Lord Jesus Christ, in that you have welcomed the models of true Love, and have helped on their way, as opportunity was given you, those men who are bound in fetters which become the saints, which are indeed the diadems of the true elect of God and of our Lord. ²And I also rejoice because the firm root of your faith, famous from the earliest times, still abides and bears fruit for our Lord Jesus Christ, who endured for our sins even to face death, "whom God raised up, having loosed the pangs of Hades." ³In him, "though you have not seen him, you believe with inexpressible and exalted joy"—joy that many have longed to experience—knowing that "you are saved by grace, not because of works," namely, by the will of God through Jesus Christ.

2 "Therefore, girding your loins, serve God in fear" and in truth, forsaking empty talkativeness and the erroneous teaching of the crowd, "believing on him who raised our Lord Jesus Christ from the dead and gave him glory" and a throne on his right hand; "to whom he subjected all things, whether in heaven or on earth," whom "everything that breathes" serves, who will come as "judge of the living and the dead," whose blood God will require from those who disobey him. 2For "he who raised him from the dead will raise us also," if we do his will and follow his commandments, and love what he loved, refraining from all wrongdoing, avarice, love of money, slander, and false witness; "not returning evil for evil or abuse for abuse," or blow for blow, or curse for curse; but rather remembering what the Lord said when he taught: 3"Judge not, that you be not judged; forgive, and you will be forgiven; be merciful, that you may be shown mercy; the measure you give will be the measure you get"; and "blessed are the poor and those persecuted for righteousness' sake, for theirs is the Kingdom of God."

3 I write these things about righteousness, brethren, not at my own instance, but because you first invited me to do so. 2Certainly, neither I nor anyone like me can follow the wisdom of the blessed and glorious Paul, who, when he was present among you face to face with the generation of his time, taught you accurately and firmly "the word of truth." Also when absent he wrote you letters that will enable you, if you study them carefully, to grow in the faith delivered to you— ³"which is a mother of us all," accompanied by hope, and led by love to God and Christ and our neighbor. For if anyone is occupied in these, he has fulfilled the commandment of righteousness; for he who possesses love is far from all sin.

4 But "the love of money is the beginning of all evils." Knowing, therefore, that "we brought nothing into the world, and we cannot take anything out," let us arm ourselves "with the weapons of righteousness," and let us first of all teach ourselves to live by the commandment of the Lord.

²Then you must teach your wives in the faith delivered to them and in love and purity—to cherish their own husbands in all fidelity, and to love all others equally in all chastity, and to educate their children in the fear of God. ³And the widows should be discreet in their faith pledged to the Lord, praying unceasingly on behalf of all, refraining from all slander, gossip, false witness, love of money—in fact, from evil of any kind—knowing that they are God's altar, that everything is examined for blemishes, and nothing escapes him whether of thoughts or sentiments, or any of "the secrets of the heart."

5 Knowing, then, that "God is not mocked," we ought to live worthily of his commandment and glory. ²Likewise the deacons should be blameless before his righteousness, as servants of God and Christ and not of men; not slanderers, or double-tongued, not lovers of money, temperate in all matters, compassionate, careful, living according to the truth of the Lord, who became "a servant of all"; to whom, if we are pleasing in the present age, we shall also obtain the age to come, inasmuch as he promised to raise us from the dead. And if we bear our citizenship worthy of him, "we shall also reign with him" —provided, of course, that we have faith. ³Similarly also the younger ones must be blameless in all things, especially taking thought of purity and bridling themselves from all evil. It is a fine thing to cut oneself off from the lusts that are in the world, for "every passion of the flesh wages war against the Spirit," and "neither fornicators nor the effeminate nor homosexuals will inherit the Kingdom of God, "nor those who do perverse things." Wherefore it is necessary to refrain from all these things, and be obedient to the presbyters and deacons as unto God and Christ. And the young women must live with blameless and pure conscience.

6 Also the presbyters must be compassionate, merciful to all, turning back those who have gone astray, looking after the sick, not neglecting widow or orphan or one that is poor; but "always taking thought for what is honorable in the sight of God and of men," refraining from all anger, partiality, unjust judgment, keeping far from all love of money, not hastily believing evil of anyone, nor being severe in judgment, knowing that we all owe the debt of sin. ²If, then, we pray the Lord to forgive us, we ourselves ought also to forgive; for we are before the eyes of the Lord and God, and "everyone shall stand before the judgment seat of

Christ and every one of us shall give an account of himself." ³So then let us "serve him with fear and all reverence," as he himself has commanded, and also the apostles who preached the gospel to us and the prophets who foretold the coming of the Lord. Let us be zealous for that which is good, refraining from occasions of scandal and from false brethren, and those who bear in hypocrisy the name of the Lord, who deceive empty-headed people.

7 For "whosoever does not confess that Jesus Christ has come in the flesh is antichrist" and whosoever does not confess the testimony of the cross "is of the devil"; and whosoever perverts the sayings of the Lord to suit his own lusts and says there is neither resurrection nor judgment—such a one is the first-born of Satan. ²Let us, therefore, forsake the vanity of the crowd and their false teachings and turn back to the word delivered to us from the beginning, "watching unto prayer" and continuing steadfast in fasting, beseeching fervently the all-seeing God "to lead us not into temptation," even as the Lord said, "The spirit indeed is willing, but the flesh is weak."

8 Let us, then, hold steadfastly and unceasingly to our Hope and to the Pledge of our righteousness, that is, Christ Jesus, "who bore our sins in his own body on the tree, who committed no sin, neither was guile found on his lips"; but for our sakes he endured everything that we might live in him. ²Therefore let us be imitators of his patient endurance, and if we suffer for the sake of his name, let us glorify him. "For he set us this example" in his own Person, and this is what we believed.

9 Now I exhort all of you to be obedient to the word of righteousness "and to exercise all patient endurance," such as you have seen with your very eyes, not only in the blessed Ignatius and Zosimus and Rufus, but also in others who were of your membership, and in Paul himself and the rest of the apostles; [2]being persuaded that all these "did not run in vain," but in faith and righteousness, and that they are now in their deserved place with the Lord, in whose suffering they also shared. For they "loved not this present world," but Him who died on our behalf and was raised by God for our sakes.

10 Stand firm, therefore, in these things and follow the example of the Lord, "steadfast and immovable" in the faith, "loving the brotherhood," "cherishing one another" "fellow companions in the truth;" in gentleness of the Lord "preferring one another" and despising no one. [2]Whenever you are able to do a kindness, "do not put it off," because "almsgiving frees from death." All of you submit yourselves to one another, having your manner of life above reproach from the heathen, so that you may receive praise for your good works and the Lord may not be blasphemed on your account. [3]Woe to them, however, through whom the name of the Lord is blasphemed." Therefore, all of you teach the sobriety in which you are yourselves living.

11 I have been exceedingly grieved on account of Valens, who was sometime a presbyter among you, because he so forgot the office that was given him. I warn you, therefore, to refrain from the love of money and be pure and truthful. [2]Shun evil of every kind. For how shall he who cannot govern himself in these things teach another? If anyone does not refrain from the love of money he will be defiled by idolatry and so be judged as if he were one of the heathen, who are ignorant of the judgment of the Lord." Or "do we not know that the saints will judge the world," as Paul teaches? However, I have neither observed nor heard of any such thing among you, with whom blessed Paul labored and who were his epistles in the beginning. Of you he has wont to boast in all the churches which at that time alone knew God; for we did not as yet know him. [4]I am, therefore, very grieved indeed for that man and his wife. "May the Lord grant them true repentance." But you, too, must be moderate in this matter; and "do not consider such persons as enemies," but reclaim them as suffering and straying members, in order that you may save the whole body of you. For in doing this you will edify yourselves.

12 I am confident indeed that you are well versed in the sacred Scriptures and that nothing escapes you—something not granted to me—only, as it is said in these Scriptures, "be angry but sin not" and "let not the sun go down on your anger." Blessed is he who remembers this. I believe it is so with you. [2]May God and the Father of our Lord Jesus Christ, build you up in faith and truth in all gentles, without anger and in patient endurance, in long-suffering, forbearance, and purity; and give you a portion and share among his saints, and to us also along with you, and to all under heaven who are destined to believe in our Lord Jesus Christ and in "his Father who raised him from the dead." [3]"Pray for all the saints." "Pray also for emperors and magistrates and rulers," and for "those who persecute and hate you," and for "the enemies of the cross," that your fruit may be manifest in all, so that you may be perfected in him.

13 Both you and Ignatius have written me that if anyone is leaving for Syria he should take your letter along too. I shall attend to this is I have a favorable opportunity—either myself or one whom I shall send to represent you as well as me. ²We are sending you the letters of Ignatius, those he addressed to us and any others we had by us, just as you requested. They are herewith appended to this letter. From them you can derive great benefit, for they are concerned with faith and patient endurance and all the edification pertaining to the Lord. Of Ignatius himself and those who are with him, let us have any reliable information that you know.

14 I am sending you this letter by Crescens, whom I recently commended to you and now commend him again. He has lived with us blamelessly, and I believe he will do so among you. I also commend to you his sister, when she arrives among you. Farewell in the Lord Jesus Christ in grace, both you and all who are yours. Amen.

The Martyrdom of Saint Polycarp, Bishop of Smyrna, as Told in the Letter of the Church of Smyrna to the Church of Philomelium

∽

THE TEXT

THE CHURCH OF GOD that sojourns at Smyrna to the church of God that sojourns at Philomelium, and to all those of the holy and Catholic Church who sojourn in every place: may mercy, peace, and love be multiplied from God the Father and our Lord Jesus Christ.

1 We write you, brethren, the things concerning those who suffered martyrdom, especially the blessed Polycarp, who put an end to the persecution by sealing it, so to speak, through his own witness. For almost everything that led up to it happened in order that the Lord might show once again a martyrdom conformable to the gospel. [2]For he waited to be betrayed, just as the Lord did, to the end that we also might be imitators of him, "not looking only to that which concerns ourselves, but also to that which concerns our neighbors." For it is a mark of true and steadfast love for one not only to desire to be saved oneself, but all the brethren also.

2 Blessed and noble, indeed, are all the martyrdoms that have taken place according to God's will; for we ought to be very reverent in ascribing to God power over all things. ²For who would not admire their nobility and patient endurance and love of their Master? Some of them, so torn by scourging that the anatomy of their flesh was visible as far as the inner veins and arteries, endured with such patience that even the bystanders took pity and wept; others achieved such heroism that not one of them uttered a cry or a groan, thus showing all of us that at the very hour of their tortures the most noble martyrs of Christ were no longer in the flesh, but rather that the Lord stood by them and conversed with them. ³And giving themselves over to the grace of Christ they despised the tortures of this world, purchasing for themselves in the space of one hour the life eternal. To them the fire of their inhuman tortures was cold; for they set before their eyes "escape from the fire that is everlasting and never quenched," while with the eyes of their heart they gazed upon the good things reserved for those that endure patiently, "which things neither ear has heard nor eye has seen, nor has there entered into the heart of man." But they were shown to them by the Lord, for they were no longer men, but were already angels. ⁴Similarly, those condemned to the wild beasts endured fearful punishments, being made to lie on sharp shells and punished with other forms of various torments, in order that [the devil] might bring them, if possible, by means of the prolonged punishment, to a denial of their faith.

3 Many, indeed, were the machinations of the devil against them. But, thanks be to God, he did not prevail against them all. For the most noble Germanicus encouraged their timidity through his own patient endurance—who also fought with the beasts in a distinguished way. For when the proconsul, wishing to persuade him, bade him have pity on his youth, he forcibly dragged the wild beast toward himself, wishing to obtain more quickly a release from their wicked and lawless life. 2From this circumstance, all the crowd, marveling at the heroism of the God-loving and God-fearing race of the Christians, shouted: "Away with the atheists! Make search for Polycarp!"

4 But a Phrygian, named Quintus, lately arrived from Phrygia, took fright when he saw the wild beasts. In fact, he was the one who had forced himself and some others to come forward voluntarily. The proconsul by much entreaty persuaded him to take the oath and to offer the sacrifice. For this reason, therefore, brethren, we do not praise those who come forward of their own accord, since the gospel does not teach us so to do.

5 The most admirable Polycarp, when he first heard of it, was not perturbed, but desired to remain in the city. But the majority induced him to withdraw, so he retired to a farm not far from the city and there stayed with a few friends, doing nothing else night and day but pray for all men and for the churches throughout the world, as was his constant habit. ²And while he was praying, it so happened, three days before his arrest, that he had a vision and saw his pillow blazing with fire, and turning to those who were with him he said, "I must be burned alive."

6 And while those who were searching for him continued their quest, he moved to another farm, and forthwith those searching for him arrived. And when they did not find him, they seized two young slaves, one of whom confessed under torture. ²For it was really impossible to conceal him, since the very ones who betrayed him were of his own household. And the chief of the police, who chanced to have the same name as Herod, was zealous to bring him into the arena in order that he might fulfill his own appointed lot of being made a partaker with Christ; while those who betrayed him should suffer the punishment of Judas himself.

7 Taking, therefore, the young slave on Friday about supper-time, the police, mounted and with their customary arms, set out as though "hasting after a robber." And late in the evening they came up with him and found him in bed in the upper room of a small cottage. Even so he could have escaped to another farm, but he did not wish to do so, saying, "God's will be done." ²Thus, when he heard of their arrival, he went downstairs and talked with them, while those who looked on marveled at his age and constancy, and at how there should be such zeal over the arrest of so old a man. Straightway he ordered food and drink, as much as they wished, to be set before them at that hour, and he asked

them to give him an hour so that he might pray undisturbed. [3]And when they consented, he stood and prayed—being so filled with the grace of God that for two hours he could not hold his peace, to the amazement of those who heard. And many repented that they had come to get such a devout old man.

8 When at last he had finished his prayer, in which he remembered all who had met with him at any time, both small and great, both those with and those without renown, and the whole Catholic Church throughout the world, the hour of departure having come, they mounted him on an ass and brought him into the city. [2]It was a great Sabbath. And there the chief of the police, Herod, and his father, Nicetas, met him and transferred him to their carriage, and tried to persuade him, as they sat beside him, saying, "What harm is there to say 'Lord Caesar,' and to offer incense and all that sort of thing, and to save yourself?" At first he did not answer them. But when they persisted, he said, "I am not going to do what you advise me." [3]Then when they failed to persuade him, they uttered dire threats and made him get out with such speed that in dismounting from the carriage he bruised his shin. But without turning around, as though nothing had happened, he proceeded swiftly, and was led into the arena, there being such a tumult in the arena that no one could be heard.

9 But as Polycarp was entering the arena, a voice from heaven came to him, saying, "Be strong, Polycarp, and play the man." No one saw the one speaking, but those of our people who were present heard the voice.

And when finally he was brought up, there was a great tumult on hearing that Polycarp had been arrested. 2Therefore, when he was brought before him, the proconsul asked him if he were Polycarp. And when he confessed that he was, he tried to persuade him to deny [the faith], saying, "Have respect to your age"—and other things that customarily follow this, such as, "Swear by the fortune of Caesar; change your mind; say, 'Away with the atheists!'"

But Polycarp looked with earnest face at the whole crowd of lawless heathen in the arena, and motioned to them with his hand. Then, groaning and looking up to heaven, he said, "Away with the atheists!"

3But the proconsul was insistent and said: "Take the oath, and I shall release you. Curse Christ."

Polycarp said: "Eighty-six years I have served him, and he never did me any wrong. How can I blaspheme my King who saved me?"

10 And upon his persisting still and saying, "Swear by the fortune of Caesar," he answered, "If you vainly suppose that I shall swear by the fortune of Caesar, as you say, and pretend that you do not know who I am, listen plainly: I am a Christian. But if you desire to learn the teaching of Christianity, appoint a day and give me a hearing."

2The proconsul said, "Try to persuade the people."

But Polycarp said, "You, I should deem worthy of an account; for we have been taught to render honor, as is befitting, to rulers and authorities appointed by God so far as it does us no harm; but as for these, I do not consider them worthy that I should make defense to them."

11 But the proconsul said: "I have wild beasts. I shall throw you to them, if you do not change your mind."

But he said: "Call them. For repentance from the better to the worse is not permitted us; but it is noble to change from what is evil to what is righteous."

2And again [he said] to him, "I shall have you consumed with fire, if you despise the wild beasts, unless you change your mind."

But Polycarp said: "The fire you threaten burns but an hour and is quenched after a little; for you do not know the fire of the coming judgment and everlasting punishment that is laid up for the impious. But why do you delay? Come, do what you will."

12 And when he had said these things and many more besides he was inspired with courage and joy, and his face was full of grace, so that not only did it not fall with dismay at the things said to him, but on the contrary, the proconsul was astonished, and sent his own herald into the midst of the arena to proclaim three times: "Polycarp has confessed himself to be a Christian."

2When this was said by the herald, the entire crowd of heathen and Jews who lived in Smyrna shouted with uncontrollable anger and a great cry: "This one is the teacher of Asia, the father of the Christians, the destroyer of our gods, who teaches many not to sacrifice nor to worship."

Such things they shouted and asked the Asiarch Philip that he let loose a lion on Polycarp. But he said it was not possible for him to do so, since he had brought the wild-beast sports to a close. ³Then they decided to shout with one accord that he burn Polycarp alive. For it was necessary that the vision which had appeared to him about his pillow should be fulfilled, when he saw it burning while he was praying, and turning around had said prophetically to the faithful who were with him, "I must be burned alive."

13 Then these things happened with such dispatch, quicker than can be told—the crowds in so great a hurry to gather wood and faggots from the workshops and the baths, the Jews being especially zealous, as usual, to assist with this. ²When the fire was ready, and he had divested himself of all his clothes and unfastened his belt, he tried to take off his shoes, though he was not heretofore in the habit of doing this because [each of] the faithful always vied with one another as to which of them would be first to touch his body. For he had always been honored, even before his martyrdom, for his holy life. ³Straightway then, they set about him the material prepared for the pyre. And when they were about to nail him also, he said: "Leave me as I am. For he who grants me to endure the fire will enable me also to remain on the pyre unmoved, without the security you desire from the nails."

14 So they did not nail him, but tied him. And with his hands put behind him and tied, like a noble ram out of a great flock ready for sacrifice, a burnt offering ready and acceptable to God, he looked up to heaven and said:

"Lord God Almighty, Father of thy beloved and blessed Servant Jesus Christ, through whom we have received full knowledge of thee, 'the God of angels and powers and all creation' and of the whole race of the righteous who live in thy presence: ²I bless thee, because thou hast deemed me worthy of this day and hour, to take my part in the number of the martyrs, in the cup of thy Christ, for 'resurrection to eternal life' of soul and body in the immortality of the Holy Spirit; among whom may I be received in thy presence this day as a rich and acceptable sacrifice, just as thou hast prepared and revealed beforehand and fulfilled, thou that art the true God without any falsehood. ³For this and for everything I praise thee, I bless thee, I glorify thee, through the eternal and heavenly High Priest, Jesus Christ, thy beloved Servant, through whom be glory to thee with him and Holy Spirit both now and unto the ages to come. Amen."

15 And when he had concluded the Amen and finished his prayer, the men attending to the fire lighted it. And when the flame flashed forth, we saw a miracle, we to whom it was given to see. And we are preserved in order to relate to the rest what happened. ²For the fire made the shape of a vaulted chamber, like a ship's sail filled by the wind, and made a wall around the body of the martyr. And he was in the midst, not as burning flesh, but as bread baking or as gold and silver refined in a furnace. And we perceived such a sweet aroma as the breath of incense or some other precious spice.

16 At length, when the lawless men saw that his body could not be consumed by the fire, they commanded an executioner to go to him and stab him with a dagger. And when he did this [a dove and] a great quantity of blood came forth, so that the fire was quenched and the whole crowd marveled that there should be such a difference between the unbelievers and the elect. 2And certainly the most admirable Polycarp was one of these [elect], in whose times among us he showed himself an apostolic and prophetic teacher and bishop of the Catholic Church in Smyrna. Indeed, every utterance that came from his mouth was accomplished and will be accomplished.

17 But the jealous and malicious evil one, the adversary of the race of the righteous, seeing the greatness of his martyrdom and his blameless life from the beginning, and how he was crowned with the wreath of immortality and had borne away an incontestable reward, so contrived it that his corpse should not be taken away by us, although many desired to do this and to have fellowship with his holy flesh. 2He instigated Nicetas, the father of Herod and brother of Alce, to plead with the magistrate not to give up his body, "else," said he, "they will abandon the Crucified and begin worshiping this one." This was done at the instigation and insistence of the Jews, who also watched when we were going to take him from the fire, being ignorant that we can never forsake Christ, who suffered for the salvation of the whole world of those who are saved, the faultless for the sinners, nor can we ever worship any other. 3For we worship this One as Son of God, but we love the martyrs as disciples and imitators of the Lord, deservedly so, because of their unsurpassable devotion to their own King and Teacher. May it be also our lot to be their companions and fellow disciples!

18 The captain of the Jews, when he saw their contentiousness, set it [i.e., his body] in the midst and burned it, as was their custom. ²So we later took up his bones, more precious than costly stones and more valuable than gold, and laid them away in a suitable place. ³There the Lord will permit us, so far as possible, to gather together in joy and gladness to celebrate the day of his martyrdom as a birthday, in memory of those athletes who have gone before, and to train and make ready those who are to come hereafter.

19 Such are the things concerning the blessed Polycarp, who, martyred at Smyrna along with twelve others from Philadelphia, is alone remembered so much the more by everyone, that he is even spoken of by the heathen in every place. He was not only a noble teacher, but also a distinguished martyr, whose martyrdom all desire to imitate as one according to the gospel of Christ. ²By his patient endurance he overcame the wicked magistrate and so received the crown of immortality; and he rejoices with the apostles and all the righteous to glorify God the Father Almighty and to bless our Lord Jesus Christ, the Savior of our souls and Helmsman of our bodies and Shepherd of the Catholic Church throughout the world.

20 You requested, indeed, that these things be related to you more fully, but for the present we have briefly reported them through our brother Marcion. When you have informed your-selves of these things, send this letter to the brethren elsewhere, in order that they too might glorify the Lord, who makes his choices from his own servants. ²To him who is able by his grace and bounty to bring us to his everlasting Kingdom, through his Servant, the only-begotten Jesus Christ, be glory, honor, might, majesty, throughout the ages. Greet all the saints. Those with us greet you and also Evarestus, who wrote this, with his whole household.

21 The blessed Polycarp was martyred on the second day of the first part of the month Xanthicus, the seventh day before the kalends of March, a great Sabbath, at two o'clock P.M. He was arrested by Herod, when Philip of Tralles was high priest, and Statius Quadratus was proconsul, but in the everlasting reign of our Lord Jesus Christ. To him be glory, honor, majesty, and the eternal throne, from generation to generation. Amen.

22 We bid you farewell, brethren, as you live by the word of Jesus Christ according to the gospel, with whom be glory to God the Father and Holy Spirit, unto the salvation of his holy elect; just as the blessed Polycarp suffered martyrdom, in whose foot-steps may it be our lot to be found in the Kingdom of Jesus Christ.

²These things Gaius copied from the papers of Irenaeus, a dis-ciple of Polycarp; he also lived with Irenaeus. And Isocrates, wrote it in Corinth from the copy of Gaius. Grace be with all.

³I, Pionius, again wrote it from the aforementioned copy, having searched for it according to a revelation of the blessed

Polycarp, who appeared to me, as I shall explain in the sequel. I gathered it together when it was almost worn out with age, in order that the Lord Jesus Christ might bring me also with his elect unto his heavenly Kingdom. To him be glory with the Father and Holy Spirit unto the ages of ages. Amen.

ANOTHER EPILOGUE
FROM THE MOSCOW MANUSCRIPT

23 These things Gaius copied from the papers of Irenaeus. He also lived with Irenaeus, who had been a disciple of the holy Polycarp. [2]For this Irenaeus, at the time of the martyrdom of Bishop Polycarp, was in Rome and taught many; and many of his excellent and orthodox writings are in circulation, in which he mentions Polycarp, for he was taught by him. He ably refuted every heresy and handed down the ecclesiastical and Catholic rule, as he had received it from the saint. [3]He says this also: that once when Marcion, after whom the Marcionites are called, met the holy Polycarp and said, "Do you know us, Polycarp?" he said to Marcion, "I know you; I know the first-born of Satan." [4]And this fact is also found in the writings of Irenaeus, that on the day and at the hour when Polycarp was martyred in Smyrna, Irenaeus, being in the city of Rome, heard a voice like a trumpet saying, "Polycarp has suffered martyrdom."

[5]From these papers of Irenaeus, then, as was said above, Gaius made a copy, and from Gaius' copy Isocrates made another in Corinth. And I, Pionius, again from the copies of Isocrates

wrote according to the revelation of holy Polycarp, when I searched for it, and gathered it together when it was almost worn out with age, in order that the Lord Jesus Christ might bring me with his elect unto his heavenly Kingdom. To whom be glory with the Father and the Son and the Holy Spirit unto the ages of ages. Amen.

The Teaching of
the Twelve Apostles,
Commonly Called
the Didache

∽

THE TEXT

THE LORD'S TEACHING to the Heathen by the Twelve Apostles:

1 There are two ways, one of life and one of death; and between the two ways there is a great difference.

²Now, this is the way of life: "First, you must love God who made you, and second, your neighbor as yourself." And whatever you want people to refrain from doing to you, you must not do to them.

³What these maxims teach is this: "Bless those who curse you," and "pray for your enemies." Moreover, fast "for those who persecute you." For "what credit is it to you if you love those who love you? Is that not the way the heathen act?" But "you must love those who hate you," and then you will make no enemies. ⁴"Abstain from carnal passions." If someone strikes you

"on the right cheek, turn to him the other too, and you will be perfect." If someone "forces you to go one mile with him, go along with him for two"; if someone robs you "of your overcoat, give him your suit as well." If someone deprives you of "your property, do not ask for it back." (You could not get it back anyway!) 5"Give to everybody who begs from you, and ask for no return." For the Father wants his own gifts to be universally shared. Happy is the man who gives as the commandment bids him, for he is guiltless! But alas for the man who receives! If he receives because he is in need, he will be guiltless. But if he is not in need he will have to stand trial why he received and for what purpose. He will be thrown into prison and have his action investigated; and "he will not get out until he has paid back the last cent." 6Indeed, there is a further saying that relates to this: "Let your donation sweat in your hands until you know to whom to give it."

2 The second commandment of the Teaching: 2"Do not murder; do not commit adultery"; do not corrupt boys; do not fornicate; "do not steal"; do not practice magic; do not go in for sorcery; do not murder a child by abortion or kill a new-born infant. "Do not covet your neighbor's property; 3do not commit perjury; do not bear false witness"; do not slander; do not bear grudges. 4Do not be double-minded or double- tongued, for a double tongue is "a deadly snare." 5Your words shall not be dishonest or hollow, but substantiated by action. 6Do not be greedy or extortionate or hypocritical or malicious or arrogant. Do not plot against your neighbor. 7Do not hate anybody; but reprove some, pray for others, and still others love more than your own life.

3 My child, flee from all wickedness and from everything of that sort. 2Do not be irritable, for anger leads to murder. Do not be jealous or contentious or impetuous, for all this breeds murder.

3My child, do not be lustful, for lust leads to fornication. Do not use foul language or leer, for all this breeds adultery.

4My child, do not be a diviner, for that leads to idolatry. Do not be an enchanter or an astrologer or a magician. Moreover, have no wish to observe or heed such practices, for all this breeds idolatry.

5My child, do not be a liar, for lying leads to theft. Do not be avaricious or vain, for all this breeds thievery.

6My child, do not be a grumbler, for grumbling leads to blasphemy. Do not be stubborn or evil-minded, for all this breeds blasphemy.

7But be humble since "the humble will inherit the earth." 8Be patient, merciful, harmless, quiet, and good; and always "have respect for the teaching" you have been given. Do not put on airs or give yourself up to presumptuousness. Do not associate with the high and mighty; but be with the upright and humble. Accept whatever happens to you as good, in the realization that nothing occurs apart from God.

4 My child, day and night "you should remember him who preaches God's word to you," and honor him as you would the Lord. For where the Lord's nature is discussed, there the Lord is.

²Every day you should seek the company of saints to enjoy their refreshing conversation. ³You must not start a schism, but reconcile those at strife. "Your judgments must be fair." You must not play favorites when reproving transgressions. ⁴You must not be of two minds about your decision.

⁵Do not be one who holds his hand out to take, but shuts it when it comes to giving. ⁶If your labor has brought you earnings, pay a ransom for your sins. ⁷Do not hesitate to give and do not give with a bad grace; for you will discover who He is that pays you back a reward with a good grace. ⁸Do not turn your back on the needy, but share everything with your brother and call nothing your own. For if you have what is eternal in common, how much more should you have what is transient!

⁹Do not neglect your responsibility to your son or your daughter, but from their youth you shall teach them to revere God. ¹⁰Do not be harsh in giving orders to your slaves. Do not give orders in anger to your handmaids and slave girls. They hope in the same God as you, and the result may be that they cease to revere the God over you both. For when he comes to call us, he will not respect our station, but will call those whom the Spirit has made ready. ¹¹You slaves, for your part, must obey your masters with reverence and fear, as if they represented God.

¹²You must hate all hypocrisy and everything which fails to please the Lord. ¹³You must not forsake "the Lord's commandments," but "observe" the ones you have been given, "neither adding nor subtracting" anything. ¹⁴At the church meeting you

must confess your sins, and not approach prayer with a bad conscience. That is the way of life.

5 But the way of death is this: First of all, it is wicked and thoroughly blasphemous: murders, adulteries, lusts, fornications, thefts, idolatries, magic arts, sorceries, robberies, false witness, hypocrisies, duplicity, deceit, arrogance, malice, stubbornness, greediness, filthy talk, jealousy, audacity, haughtiness, boastfulness.

²Those who persecute good people, who hate truth, who love lies, who are ignorant of the reward of uprightness, who do not "abide by goodness" or justice, and are on the alert not for goodness but for evil: gentleness and patience are remote from them. "They love vanity, " "look for profit," have no pity for the poor, do not exert themselves for the oppressed, ignore their Maker, "murder children," corrupt God's image, turn their backs on the needy, oppress the afflicted, defend the rich, unjustly condemn the poor, and are thoroughly wicked. My children, may you be saved from all this!

6 See "that no one leads you astray" from this way of the teaching, since such a one's teaching is godless.

²If you can bear the Lord's full yoke, you will be perfect. But if you cannot, then do what you can.

³Now about food: undertake what you can. But keep strictly away from what is offered to idols, for that implies worshiping dead gods.

7 Now about baptism: this is how to baptize. Give public instruction on all these points, and then "baptize" in running water, "in the name of the Father and of the Son and of the Holy Spirit." 2If you do not have running water, baptize in some other. 3If you cannot in cold, then in warm. If you have neither, then pour water on the head three times "in the name of the Father, Son, and Holy Spirit." 4Before the baptism, moreover, the one who baptizes and the one being baptized must fast, and any others who can. And you must tell the one being baptized to fast for one or two days beforehand.

8 Your fasts must not be identical with those of the hypocrites. They fast on Mondays and Thursdays; but you should fast on Wednesdays and Fridays.

2You must not pray like the hypocrites, but "pray as follows" as the Lord bid us in his gospel: "Our Father in heaven, hallowed be your name; your Kingdom come; your will be done on earth as it is in heaven; give us today our bread for the morrow; and forgive us our debts as we forgive our debtors. And do not lead us into temptation, but save us from the evil one, for yours is the power and the glory forever."

3You should pray in this way three times a day.

9 Now about the Eucharist: This is how to give thanks: 2First in connection with the cup: "We thank you, our Father, for the holy vine"' of David, your child, which you have revealed through Jesus, your child. To you be glory forever."

3Then in connection with the piece [broken off the loaf]:

"We thank you, our Father, for the life and knowledge which you have revealed through Jesus, your child. To you be glory forever.

⁴"As this piece [of bread] was scattered over the hills and then was brought together and made one, so let your Church be brought together from the ends of the earth into your Kingdom. For yours is the glory and the power through Jesus Christ forever."

⁵You must not let anyone eat or drink of your Eucharist except those baptized in the Lord's name. For in reference to this the Lord said, "Do not give what is sacred to dogs."

10 After you have finished your meal, say grace in this way:

²"We thank you, holy Father, for your sacred name which you have lodged in our hearts, and for the knowledge and faith and immortality which you have revealed through Jesus, your child. To you be glory forever.

³"Almighty Master, 'you have created everything' for the sake of your name, and have given men food and drink to enjoy that they may thank you. But to us you have given spiritual food and drink and eternal life through Jesus, your child.

⁴"Above all, we thank you that you are mighty. To you be glory forever.

⁵"Remember, Lord, your Church, to save it from all evil and to make it perfect by your love. Make it holy, 'and gather' it 'together from the four winds' into your Kingdom which you have made ready for it. For yours is the power and the glory forever.

⁶"Let Grace come and let this world pass away.

"Hosanna to the God of David!

"If anyone is holy, let him come. If not, let him repent.

"Our Lord, come!

"Amen."

7In the case of prophets, however, you should let them give thanks in their own way.

11 Now, you should welcome anyone who comes your way and teaches you all we have been saying. A renegade and by teaching otherwise contradicts all this, pay no attention to him. 2But if his teaching furthers the Lord's righteousness and knowledge, welcome him as the Lord.

3Now about the apostles and prophets: Act in line with the gospel precept. 4Welcome every apostle on arriving, as if he were the Lord. 5But he must not stay beyond one day. In case of necessity, however, the next day too. If he stays three days, he is a false prophet. 6On departing, an apostle must not accept anything save sufficient food to carry him till his next lodging. If he asks for money, he is a false prophet.

7While a prophet is making ecstatic utterances you must not test or examine him. For "every sin will be forgiven." 8However, not everybody making ecstatic utterances is a prophet, but only if he behaves like the Lord. It is by their conduct that the false prophet and the [true] prophet can be distinguished. 9For instance, if a prophet marks out a table in the Spirit, he must not eat from it. If he does, he is a false prophet. 10Again, every prophet who teaches the truth but fails to practice what he preaches is a false prophet. 11But every attested and genuine prophet who acts with a view to symbolizing the mystery of the Church,'" and does not teach you to do all he does, must not be judged by you.

His judgment rests with God. For the ancient prophets too acted in this way. [12]But if someone says in the Spirit, "Give me money, or something else," you must not heed him. However, if he tells you to give for others in need, no one must condemn him.

12 Everyone "who comes" to you "in the name of the Lord" must be welcomed. Afterward, when you have tested him, you will find out about him, for you have insight into right and wrong. [2]If it is a traveler who arrives, help him all you can. But he must not stay with you more than two days, or, if necessary, three. [3]If he wants to settle with you and is an artisan, he must work for his living. [4]If, however, he has no trade, use your judgment in taking steps for him to live with you as a Christian without being idle. [5]If he refuses to do this, he is trading on Christ. You must be on your guard against such people.

13 Every genuine prophet who wants to settle with you "has a right to his support." [2]Similarly, a genuine teacher himself, just like a "workman, has a right to his support." [3]Hence take all the first fruits of vintage and harvest, and of cattle and sheep, and give these first fruits to the prophets. For they are your high priests. [4]If, however, you have no prophet, give them to the poor. [5]If you make bread, take the first fruits and give in accordance with the precept. [6]Similarly, when you open a jar of wine or oil, take the first fruits and give them to the prophets. [7]Indeed, of money, clothes, and of all your possessions, take such first fruits as you think right, and give in accordance with the precept.

14 On every Lord's Day—his special day—come together and break bread and give thanks, first confessing your sins so that your sacrifice may be pure. ²Anyone at variance with his neighbor must not join you, until they are reconciled, lest your sacrifice be defiled. ³For it was of this sacrifice that the Lord said, "Always and everywhere offer me a pure sacrifice; for I am a great King, says the Lord, and my name is marveled at by the nations."

15 You must, then, elect for yourselves bishops and deacons who are credit to the Lord, men who are gentle, generous, faithful, and well tried. For their ministry to you is identical with that of the prophets and teachers. ²You must not, therefore, despise them, for along with the prophets and teachers they enjoy a place of honor among you.

³Furthermore, do not reprove each other angrily, but quietly, as you find it in the gospel. Moreover, if anyone has wronged his neighbor, nobody must speak to him, and he must not hear a word from you, until he repents. ⁴Say your prayers, give your charity, and do everything just as you find it in the gospel of our Lord.

16 "Watch" over your life: do not let "your lamps" go out, and do not keep "your loins ungirded"; but "be ready," for "you do not know the hour when our Lord is coming." ²Meet together frequently in your search for what is good for your souls, since "a lifetime of faith will be of no advantage" to you unless you prove perfect at the very last. ³For in the final days multitudes of false prophets and seducers will appear. ⁴Sheep will turn into wolves, and love into hatred. For with the increase of iniquity men will hate, persecute, and betray each other. And then the world deceiver will appear in the guise of God's Son. He will work "signs and wonders" and the earth will fall into his hands and he will commit outrages such as have never occurred before. 5Then mankind will come to the fiery trial "and many will fall away" and perish, "but those who persevere" in their faith "will be saved by the Curse himself." 6Then "there will appear the signs of the Truth: first the sign of stretched-out [hands] in heaven, then the sign of "a trumpet's blast," and thirdly the resurrection of the dead, though not of all the dead, 7but as it has been said: "The Lord will come and all his saints with him. Then the world will see the Lord coming on the clouds of the sky."

THE PASTOR OF HERMAS

THE PASTOR
FIRST BOOK—VISIONS

First Vision
Against Filthy and
Proud Thoughts, and the
Carelessness of Hermas in
Chastising His Sons

ᴄᴠ

Chapter 1

HE WHO HAD BROUGHT me up, sold me to one Rhode in Rome. Many years after this I recognised her, and I began to love her as a sister. Some time after, I saw her bathe in the river Tiber; and I gave her my hand, and drew her out of the river. The sight of her beauty made me think with myself, "I should be a happy man if I could but get a wife as handsome and good as she is." This was the only thought that passed through me: this and nothing more. A short time after this, as I was walking on my road to the villages, and magnifying the creatures of God, and thinking how magnificent, and beautiful, and powerful they are, I fell asleep. And the Spirit carried me away, and took me through a pathless place, through which a man could not travel, for it was situated in the midst of rocks; it rugged and impassible on account of water. Having passed over this river, I came to a plain. I then bent down on my knees, and began pray to the Lord, and to confess my sins. And as I prayed, the heavens were opened, and I see the woman whom I had desired saluting me from the sky, and saying, "Hail, Hermas!" And looking up to her, I said, "Lady, what doest thou here?" And she answered me, "I have been taken up here to accuse you of your sins before the Lord." "Lady," said I, "are you to be the subject of my accusation?" "No," said she; "but hear the words which I am going to speak to you. God, who dwells in the heavens, and made out of nothing the things that exist, and multiplied and increased them on account of His holy Church, is angry with you for having sinned against me." I answered her, "Lady, have I sinned against you? How or when spoke I an unseemly word to you? Did I not always think of you as a lady? Did I not always respect you as a sister? Why do you falsely accuse me of this wickedness and impurity?" With a smile she replied to me, "The desire of wickedness arose within your heart. Is it not your opinion that a righteous man commits sin when an evil desire arises in his heart? There is sin in such a case, and the sin is great," said she; "for the thoughts of a righteous man should be righteous. For by thinking righteously his character is established in the heavens, and he has the Lord merciful to him in every business. But such as entertain wicked thoughts in their minds are bringing upon themselves death and captivity; and especially is this the case with those who set their affections on this world, and glory in their riches, and look not forward to the blessings of the life to come. For many will their regrets be; for they have no hope, but have despaired of themselves and their life. But do thou pray to God, and He will heal thy sins and the sins of thy whole house, and of all the saints."

Chapter 2

After she had spoken these words, the heavens were shut. I was overwhelmed with sorrow and fear, and said to myself, "If this sin is assigned to me, how can I be saved, or how shall I propiti- ate God in regard to my sins, which are of the grossest character? With what words shall I ask the Lord to be merciful to me?" While I was thinking over these things, and discussing them in my mind, I saw opposite to me a chair, white, made of white wool, of great size. And there came up an old woman, arrayed in a splendid robe, and with a book in her hand; and she sat down alone, and saluted me, "Hail, Hermas!" And in sadness and tears I said to her, "Lady, hail!" And she said to me, "Why are you downcast, Hermas? For you were wont to be patient and temper- ate, and always smiling. Why are you so gloomy, and not cheer- ful?" I answered her and said, "O Lady, I have been reproached by a very good woman, who says that I sinned against her." And she said, "Far be such a deed from a servant of God. But perhaps a desire after her has arisen within your heart. Such a wish, in the case of the servants of God, produces sin. For it is a wicked and horrible wish in an all-chaste and already well-tried spirit to desire an evil deed; and especially for Hermas so to do, who keeps himself from all wicked desire, and is full of all simplicity, and of great guilelessness."

Chapter 3

"But God is not angry with you on account of this, but that you may convert your house, which have committed iniquity against the Lord, and against you, their parent. And although you love your sons, yet did you not warn your house, but permitted them to be terribly corrupted. On this account is the Lord angry with you, but He will heal all the evils which have been done in your house. For, on account of their sins and iniquities, you have been destroyed by the affairs of this world. But now the mercy of the Lord has taken pity on you and your house, and will strengthen you, and establish you in his glory. Only be not easy-minded, but be of good courage and comfort your house. For as a smith hammers out his work, and accomplishes whatever he wishes, so shall righteous daily speech overcome all iniquity. Cease not therefore to admonish your sons; for I know that, if they will repent with all their heart, they will be enrolled in the Books of Life with the saints. Having ended these words, she said to me, "Do you wish to hear me read?" I say to her, "Lady, I do." "Listen then, and give ear to the glories of God." And then I heard from her, magnificently and admirably, things which my memory could not retain. For all the words were terrible, such as man could not endure. The last words, however, I did remember; for they were useful to us, and gentle. "Lo, the God of powers, who by His invisible strong power and great wisdom has created the world, and by His glorious counsel has surrounded His creation with beauty, and by His strong word has fixed the heavens and laid the foundations of the earth upon the waters, and by His own wisdom and providence has created His holy Church, which He has blessed, lo! He removes the heavens and the mountains, the hills and the seas, and all things become plain to His elect, that He may bestow on them the blessing which He has promised them, with much glory and joy, if only they shall keep the commandments of God which they have received in great faith.

Chapter 4

When she had ended her reading, she rose from the chair, and four young men came and carried off the chair and went away to the east. And she called me to herself and touched my breast, and said to me, "Have you been pleased with my reading?" And I say to her, "Lady, the last words please me, but the first are cruel and harsh." Then she said to me, "The last are for the righteous: the first are for heathens and apostates." And while she spoke to me, two men appeared and raised her on their shoulders, and they went to where the chair was in the east. With joyful countenance did she depart; and as she went, she said to me, "Behave like a man, Hermas."

Second Vision
Again, of His Neglect in
Chastising His Talkative Wife
and His Lustful Sons, and of
His Character

∾

Chapter 1

AS I WAS GOING to the country about the same time as on the previous year, in my walk I recalled to memory the vision of that year. And again the Spirit carried me away, and took me to the same place where I had been the year before. On coming to that place, I bowed my knees and began to pray to the Lord, and to glorify His name, because He had deemed me worthy, and had made known to me my former sins. On rising from prayer, I see opposite me that old woman, whom I had seen the year before, walking and reading some book. And she says to me, "Can you carry a report of these things to the elect of God?" I say to her, "Lady, so much I cannot retain in my memory, but give me the book and I shall transcribe it." "Take it," says she, "and you will give it back to me." Thereupon I took it, and going away into a certain

part of the country, I transcribed the whole of it letter by letter;
but the syllables of it I did not catch. No sooner, however, had I
finished the writing of the book, than all of a sudden it was
snatched from my hands; but who the person was that snatched
it, I saw not.

Chapter 2

Fifteen days after, when I had fasted and prayed much to the Lord,
the knowledge of the writing was revealed to me. Now the writing was to this effect: "Your seed, O Hermas, has sinned against
God, and they have blasphemed against the Lord, and in their
great wickedness they have betrayed their parents. And they
passed as traitors of their parents, and by their treachery did they
not reap profit. And even now they have added to their sins lusts
and iniquitous pollutions, and thus their iniquities have been
filled up. But make known these words to all your children, and
to your wife, who is to be your sister. For she does not restrain
her tongue, with which she commits iniquity; but, on hearing
these words, she will control herself, and will obtain mercy. For
after you have made known to them these words which my Lord
has commanded me to reveal to you, then shall they be forgiven
all the sins which in former times they committed, and forgive-
ness will be granted to all the saints who have sinned even to the
present day, if they repent with all their heart, and drive all
doubts from their minds. For the Lord has sworn by His glory, in
regard to His elect, that if any one of them sin after a certain day

which has been fixed, he shall not be saved. For the repentance of the righteous has limits. Filled up are the days of repentance to all the saints; but to the heathen, repentance will be possible even to the last day. You will tell, therefore, those who preside over the Church, to direct their ways in righteousness, that they may receive in full the promises with great glory. Stand steadfast, therefore, ye who work righteousness, and doubt not, that your passage may be with the holy angels. Happy ye who endure the great tribulation that is coming on, and happy they who shall not deny their own life. For the Lord hath sworn by His Son, that those who denied their Lord have abandoned their life in despair, for even now these are to deny Him in the days that are coming. To those who denied in earlier times, God became gracious, on account of His exceeding tender mercy.

Chapter 3

"But as for you, Hermas, remember not the wrongs done to you by your children, nor neglect your sister, that they may be cleansed from their former sins. For they will be instructed with righteous instruction, if you remember not the wrongs they have done you. For the remembrance of wrongs worketh death. And you, Hermas, have endured great personal tribulations on account of the transgressions of your house, because you did not attend to them, but were careless and engaged in your wicked transactions. But you are saved, because you did not depart from the living God, and on account of your simplicity and great self-control. These have saved you, if you remain steadfast. And they will save all who act in the same manner, and walk in guilelessness and simplicity. Those who possess such virtues will wax strong against every form of wickedness, and will abide unto eternal life. Blessed are all they who practice righteousness, for they shall never be destroyed. Now you will tell Maximus: Lo! tribulation cometh on. If it seemeth good to thee, deny again. The Lord is near to them who return unto Him, as it is written in Eldad and Modat, who prophesied to the people in the wilderness."

Chapter 4

Now a revelation was given to me, my brethren, while I slept, by a young man of comely appearance, who said to me, "Who do you think that old woman is from whom you received the book?" And I said, "The Sibyl." "You are in a mistake," says he; "it is not the Sibyl." "Who is it then?" say I. And he said, "It is the Church." And I said to him, "Why then is she an old woman?" "Because," said he, "she was created first of all. On this account is she old. And for her sake was the world made." After that I saw a vision in my house, and that old woman came and asked me, if I had yet given the book to the presbyters. And I said that I had not. And then she said, "You have done well, for I have some words to add. But when I finish all the words, all the elect will then become acquainted with them through you. You will write therefore two books, and you will send the one to Clemens and the other to Grapte. And Clemens will send his to foreign countries, for permission has been granted to him to do so. And Grapte will admonish the widows and the orphans. But you will read the words in this city, along with the presbyters who preside over the Church."

Third Vision
Concerning the Building
of the Triumphant Church,
and the Various Classes
of Reprobate Men

∾

Chapter I

THE VISION WHICH I SAW, my brethren, was of the following nature. Having fasted frequently, and having prayed to the Lord that He would show me the revelation which He promised to show me through that old woman, the same night that old woman appeared to me, and said to me, "Since you are so anxious and eager to know all things, go into the part of the country where you tarry; and about the fifth hour I shall appear unto you, and show you all that you ought to see." I asked her, saying, "Lady, into what part of the country am I to go?" And she said, "Into any part you wish." Then I chose a spot which was suitable, and retired. Before, however, I began to speak and to mention the place, she said to me, "I will come where you wish." Accordingly, I went to the country, and counted the hours, and reached the place where I had promised to meet her. And I see an ivory seat ready placed, and on it a linen cushion, and above the linen cushion was spread a covering of fine linen. Seeing these laid out, and yet no one in the place, I began to feel awe, and as it were a trembling seized hold of me, and my hair stood on end, and as it were a horror came upon me when I saw that I was all alone. But on coming back to myself and calling to mind the glory of God, I took courage, bent my knees, and again confessed my sins to God as I had done before. Whereupon the old woman approached, accompanied by six young men whom I had also seen before; and she stood behind me, and listened to me, as I prayed and confessed my sins to the Lord. And touching me she said, "Hermas, cease praying continually for your sins; pray for righteousness, that you may have a portion of it immediately in your house." On this, she took me up by the hand, and brought me to the seat, and said to the young men, "Go and build." When the young men had gone and we were alone, she said to me, "Sit here." I say to her, "Lady, permit my elders to be seated first." "Do what I bid you," said she; "sit down." When I would have sat down on her right, she did not permit me, but with her hand beckoned to me to sit down on the left. While I was thinking about this, and feeling vexed that she did not let me sit on the right, she said, "Are you vexed, Hermas? The place to the right is for others who have already pleased God, and have suffered for His name's sake; and you have yet much to accomplish before you can sit with them. But abide as you now do in your simplicity, and you will sit with them, and with all who do their deeds and bear what they have borne."

Chapter 2

"What have they borne?" said I. "Listen," said she: "scourges, prisons, great tribulations, crosses, wild beasts, for God's name's sake. On this account is assigned to them the division of sanctification on the right hand, and to every one who shall suffer for God's name: to the rest is assigned the division on the left. But both for those who sit on the right, and those who sit on the left, there are the same gifts and promises; only those sit on the right, and have some glory. You then are eager to sit on the right with them, but your shortcomings are many. But you will be cleansed from your shortcomings; and all who are not given to doubts shall be cleansed from all their iniquities up till this day." Saying this, she wished to go away. But falling down at her feet, I begged her by the Lord that she would show me the vision which she had promised to show me. And then she again took hold of me by the hand, and raised me, and made me sit on the seat to the left; and lifting up a splendid rod, she said to me, "Do you see something great?" And I say, "Lady, I see nothing." She said to me, "Lo! do you not see opposite to you a great tower, built upon the waters, of splendid square stones?" For the tower was built square by those six young men who had come with her. But myriads of men were carrying stones to it, some dragging them from the depths, others removing them from the land, and they handed them to these six young men. They were taking them and building; and those of the stones that were dragged out of the depths, they placed in the building just as they were: for they were polished and fitted exactly into the other stones, and became so united one with another that the lines of juncture could not be perceived. And in this way the building of the tower looked as if it were made out of one stone. Those stones, however, which were taken from the earth suffered a different fate; for the young men rejected some of them, some they fitted into the building, and some they cut down, and cast far away from the tower. Many other stones, however, lay around the tower, and the young men did not use them in building; for some of them were rough, others had cracks in them, others had been made too short, and others were white and round, but did not fit into the building of the tower. Moreover, I saw other stones thrown far away from the tower, and falling into the public road; yet they did not remain on the road, but were rolled into a pathless place. And I saw others falling into the fire and burning, others falling close to the water, and yet not capable of being rolled into the water, though they wished to be rolled down, and to enter the water.

Chapter 3

On showing me these visions, she wished to retire. I said to her, "What is the use of my having seen all this, while I do not know what it means?" She said to me, "You are a cunning fellow, wishing to know everything that relates to the tower." "Even so, O

Lady," said I, "that I may tell it to my brethren, that, hearing this, they may know the Lord in much glory." And she said, "Many indeed shall hear, and hearing, some shall be glad, and some shall weep. But even these, if they hear and repent, shall also rejoice. Hear, then, the parables of the tower; for I will reveal all to you, and give me no more trouble in regard to revelation: for these revelations have an end, for they have been completed. But you will not cease praying for revelations, for you are shameless. The tower which you see building is myself, the Church, who have appeared to you now and on the former occasion. Ask, then, whatever you like in regard to the tower, and I will reveal it to you, that you may rejoice with the saints." I said unto her, "Lady, since you have vouchsafed to reveal all to me this once, reveal it." She said to me, "Whatsoever ought to be revealed, will be revealed; only let your heart be with God, and doubt not whatsoever you shall see." I asked her, "Why was the tower built upon the waters, O Lady?" She answered, "I told you before, and you still inquire carefully: therefore inquiring you shall find the truth. Hear then why the tower is built upon the waters. It is because your life has been, and will be, saved through water. For the tower was founder on the word of the almighty and glorious Name and it is kept together by the invisible power of the Lord."

Chapter 4

In reply I said to her, "This is magnificent and marvellous. But who are the six young men who are engaged in building?" And

she said,"These are the holy angels of God, who were first created, and to whom the Lord handed over His whole creation, that
they might increase and build up and rule over the whole creation. By these will the building of the tower be finished." "But
who are the other persons who are engaged in carrying the
stones?" "These also are holy angels of the Lord, but the former
six are more excellent than these. The building of the tower will
be finished, and all will rejoice together around the tower, and
they will glorify God, because the tower is finished." I asked her,
saying, "Lady, I should like to know what became of the stones,
and what was meant by the various kinds of stones?" In reply she
said to me, "Not because you are more deserving than all others
that this revelation should be made to you—for there are others
before you, and better than you, to whom these visions should
have been revealed—but that the name of God may be glorified,
has the revelation been made to you, and it will be made on
account of the doubtful who ponder in their hearts whether these
things will be or not. Tell them that all these things are true, and
that none of them is beyond the truth. All of them are firm and
sure, and established on a strong foundation."

Chapter 5

"Hear now with regard to the stones which are in the building.
Those square white stones which fitted exactly into each other,
are apostles, bishops, teachers, and deacons, who have lived in
godly purity, and have acted as bishops and teachers and deacons

chastely and reverently to the elect of God. Some of them have fallen asleep, and some still remain alive. And they have always agreed with each other, and been at peace among themselves, and listened to each other. On account of this, they join exactly into the building of the tower." "But who are the stones that were dragged from the depths, and which were laid into the building and fitted in with the rest of the stones previously placed in the tower?" "They are those who suffered for the Lord's sake." "But I wish to know, O Lady, who are the other stones which were carried from the land." "Those," she said, "which go into the building without being polished, are those whom God has approved of, for they walked in the straight ways of the Lord and practiced His commandments." "But who are those who are in the act of being brought and placed in the building?" "They are those who are young in faith and are faithful. But they are admonished by the angels to do good, for no iniquity has been found in them." "Who then are those whom they rejected and cast away?" "These are they who have sinned, and wish to repent. On this account they have not been thrown far from the tower, because they will yet be useful in the building, if they repent. Those then who are to repent, if they do repent, will be strong in faith, if they now repent while the tower is building. For if the building be finished, there will not be more room for any one, but he will be rejected. This privilege, however, will belong only to him who has now been placed near the tower."

Chapter 6

"As to those who were cut down and thrown far away from the tower, do you wish to know who they are? They are the sons of iniquity, and they believed in hypocrisy, and wickedness did not depart from them. For this reason they are not saved, since they cannot be used in the building on account of their iniquities. Wherefore they have been cut off and cast far away on account of the anger of the Lord, for they have roused Him to anger. But I shall explain to you the other stones which you saw lying in great numbers, and not going into the building. Those which are rough are those who have known the truth and not remained in it, nor have they been joined to the saints. On this account are they unfit for use." "Who are those that have rents?" "These are they who are at discord in their hearts one with another, and are not at peace amongst themselves: they indeed keep peace before each other, but when they separate one from the other, their wicked thoughts remain in their hearts. These, then, are the rents which are in the stones. But those which are shortened are those who have indeed believed, and have the larger share of righteousness; yet they have also a considerable share of iniquity, and therefore they are shortened and not whole." "But who are these, Lady, that are white and round, and yet do not fit into the building of the tower?" She answered and said, "How long will you be foolish and stupid, and continue to put every kind of question and understand nothing? These are those who have faith indeed, but they have also the riches of this world. When, therefore, tribulation comes, on account of their riches and business they deny the Lord." I answered and said to her, "When, then, will they be useful for the building, Lady?" "When the riches that now seduce them have been circumscribed, then will they be of use to God. For as a round stone cannot become square unless portions be cut off and cast away, so also those who are rich in this world cannot be useful to the Lord unless their riches be cut down. Learn this first from your own case. When you were rich, you were useless; but now you are useful and fit for life. Be ye useful to God; for you also will be used as one of these stones."

Chapter 7

"Now the other stones which you saw cast far away from the tower, and falling upon the public road and rolling from it into pathless places, are those who have indeed believed, but through doubt have abandoned the true road. Thinking, then, that they could find a better, they wander and become wretched, and enter upon pathless places. But those which fell into the fire and were burned are those who have departed for ever from the living God; nor does the thought of repentance ever come into their hearts, on account of their devotion to their lusts and to the crimes which they committed. Do you wish to know who are the others which fell near the waters, but could not be rolled into them? These are they who have heard the word, and wish to be baptized in the name of the Lord; but when the chastity demanded by the truth comes into their recollection, they draw back, and again walk after their own wicked desires." She finished her exposition of the tower. But I, shameless as I yet was, asked her, "Is repentance possible for all those stones which have been cast away and did not fit into the building of the tower, and will they yet have a place in this tower?" "Repentance," said she, "is yet possible, but in this tower they cannot find a suitable place. But in another and much inferior place they will be laid, and that, too, only when they have been tortured and completed the days of their sins. And on this account will they be transferred, because they have partaken of the righteous Word. And then only will they be removed from their punishments when the thought of repenting of the evil deeds which they have done has come into their hearts. But if it does not come into their hearts, they will not be saved, on account of the hardness of their heart."

Chapter 8

When then I ceased asking in regard to all these matters, she said me, "Do you wish to see anything else?" And as I was extremely eager to see something more, my countenance beamed with joy. She looked towards me with a smile, and said, "Do you see seven women around the tower?" "I do, Lady," said I. "This tower," said she, "is supported by them according to the precept of the Lord. Listen now to their functions. The first of them, who is clasping her hands, is called Faith. Through her the elect of God are saved. Another, who has her garments tucked up and acts with vigour, is called Self-restraint. She is the daughter of Faith.

Whoever then follows her will become happy in his life, because he will restrain himself from all evil works, believing that, if he restrain himself from all evil desire, he will inherit eternal life." "But the others," said I, "O Lady, who are they?" And she said to me, "They are daughters of each other. One of them is called Simplicity, another Guilelessness, another Chastity, another Intelligence, another Love. When then you do all the works of their mother, you will be able to live." "I should like to know," said I, "O Lady, what power each one of them possesses." "Hear," she said, "what power they have. Their powers are regulated by each other, and follow each other in the order of their birth. For from Faith arises Self-restraint; from Self-restraint, Simplicity; from Simplicity, Guilelessness; from Guilelessness, Chastity; from Chastity, Intelligence; and from Intelligence, Love. The deeds, then, of these are pure, and chaste, and divine. Whoever devotes himself to these, and is able to hold fast by their works, shall have his dwelling in the tower with the saints of God." Then I asked her in regard to the ages, if now there is the conclusion. She cried out with a loud voice, "Foolish man! do you not see the tower yet building? When the tower is finished and built, then comes the end; and I assure you it will be soon finished. Ask me no more questions. Let you and all the saints be content with what I have called to your remembrance, and with my renewal of your spirits. But observe that it is not for your own sake only that these revelations have been made to you, but they have been given you that you may show them to all. For after three days—this you will take care to remember—I command you to speak all the words which I am to say to you into the ears of the saints, that hearing them and doing them, they may be cleansed from their iniquities, and you along with them."

Chapter 9

Give ear unto me, O Sons: I have brought you up in much simplicity, and guilelessness, and chastity, on account of the mercy of the Lord, who has dropped His righteousness down upon you, that ye may be made righteous and holy from all your iniquity and depravity; but you do not wish to rest from your iniquity. Now, therefore, listen to me, and be at peace one with another, and visit each other, and bear each other's burdens, and do not partake of God's creatures alone, but give abundantly of them to the needy. For some through the abundance of their food produce weakness in their flesh, and thus corrupt their flesh; while the flesh of others who have no food is corrupted, because they have not sufficient nourishment. And on this account their bodies waste away. This intemperance in eating is thus injurious to you who have abundance and do not distribute among those who are needy. Give heed to the judgment that is to come. Ye, therefore, who are high in position, seek out the hungry as long as the tower is not yet finished; for after the tower is finished, you will wish to do good, but will find no opportunity. Give heed, therefore, ye who glory in your wealth, lest those who are needy should groan, and their groans should ascend to the Lord, and ye be shut out with all your goods beyond the gate of the tower. Wherefore I now say to you who preside over the Church and love the first seats, "Be not like the drug-mixers. For the drug-mixers carry their drugs in boxes, but ye carry your drug and poison in your heart. Ye are hardened, and do not wish to cleanse your hearts, and to add unity of aim to purity of heart, you may have mercy from the great King. Take heed, therefore, children, that these dissensions of yours do not deprive you of your life. How will you instruct the elect of the Lord, if you yourselves have not instruction? Instruct each other therefore, and be at peace among yourselves, that I also, standing joyful before your Father, may give an account of you all to your Lord."

Chapter 10

On her ceasing to speak to me, those six young men who were engaged in building came and conveyed her to the tower, and other four lifted up the seat and carried it also to the tower. The faces of these last I did not see, for they were turned away from me. And as she was going, I asked her to reveal to me the meaning of the three forms in which she appeared to me. In reply she said to me: "With regard to them, you must ask another to reveal their meaning to you." For she had appeared to me, brethren, in the first vision the previous year under the form of an exceedingly old woman, sitting in a chair. In the second vision her face was youthful, but her skin and hair betokened age, and she stood while she spoke to me. She was also more joyful than on the first occasion. But in the third vision she was entirely youthful and exquisitely beautiful, except only that she had the hair of an old woman; but her face beamed with joy, and she sat on a seat. Now I was exceeding sad in regard to these appearances, for I longed much to know what the visions meant. Then I see the old woman in a vision of the night saying unto me: "Every prayer should be accompanied with humility: fast, therefore, and you will obtain from the Lord what you beg." I fasted therefore for one day.

That very night there appeared to me a young man, who said, "Why do you frequently ask revelations in prayer? Take heed lest by asking many things you injure your flesh: be content with these revelations. Will you be able to see greater revelations than those which you have seen?" I answered and said to him, "Sir, one thing only I ask, that in regard to these three forms the revelation may be rendered complete." He answered me, "How long are ye senseless? But your doubts make you senseless, because you have not your hearts turned towards the Lord." But I answered and said to him, "From you, sir, we shall learn these things more accurately."

Chapter 11

"Hear then," said he, "with regard to the three forms, concerning which you are inquiring. Why in the first vision did she appear to you as an old woman seated on a chair? Because your spirit is now old and withered up, and has lost its power in consequence of your infirmities and doubts. For, like elderly men who have no hope of renewing their strength, and expect nothing but their last sleep, so you, weakened by worldly occupations, have given yourselves up to sloth, and have not cast your cares upon the Lord. Your spirit therefore is broken, and you have grown old in your sorrows." "I should like then to know, sir, why she sat on a chair?" He answered, "Because every weak person sits on a chair on account of his weakness, that his weakness may be sustained. Lo! you have the form of the first vision."

Chapter 12

"Now in the second vision you saw her standing with a youthful countenance, and more joyful than before; still she had the skin and hair of an aged woman. Hear," said he, "this parable also. When one becomes somewhat old, he despairs of himself on account of his weakness and poverty, and looks forward to nothing but the last day of his life. Then suddenly an inheritance is left him: and hearing of this, he rises up, and becoming exceeding joyful, he puts on strength. And now he no longer reclines, but stands up; and his spirit, already destroyed by his previous actions, is renewed, and he no longer sits, but acts with vigour. So happened it with you on hearing the revelation which God gave you. For the Lord had compassion on you, and renewed your spirit, and ye laid aside your infirmities. Vigour arose within you, and ye grew strong in faith; and the Lord, seeing your strength rejoiced. On this account He showed you this building of the tower; and He will show you other things, if you continue at peace with each other with all your heart."

Chapter 13

"Now, in the third vision, you saw her still younger, and she was noble and joyful, and her shape was beautiful. For, just as when some good news comes suddenly to one who is sad, immediately he forgets his former sorrows, and looks for nothing else than the good news which he has heard, and for the future is made strong for good, and his spirit is renewed on account of the joy which he has received; so ye also have received the renewal of your spirits by seeing these good things. As to your seeing her sitting on a seat, that means that her position is one of strength, for a seat has four feet and stands firmly. For the world also is kept together by means of four elements. Those, therefore, who repent completely and with the whole heart, will become young and firmly established. You now have the revelation completely given you. Make no further demands for revelations. If anything ought to be revealed, it will be revealed to you."

Fourth Vision
Concerning the
Trial and Tribulation
That Are to Come
upon Men

∾

Chapter 1

TWENTY DAYS AFTER the former vision I saw another vision,
brethren —a representation of the tribulation that is to come. I
was going to a country house along the Campanian road. Now
the house lay about ten furlongs from the public road. The dis-
trict is one rarely traversed. And as I walked alone, I prayed the
Lord to complete the revelations which He had made to me
through His holy Church, that He might strengthen me, and give
repentance to all His servants who were going astray, that His
great and glorious name might be glorified because He vouchsafed to show me His marvels. And while I was glorifying Him
and giving Him thanks, a voice, as it were, answered me, "Doubt
not, Hermas;" and I began to think with myself, and to say,
"What reason have I to doubt—I who have been established by

the Lord, and who have seen such glorious sights?" I advanced a little, brethren, and, lo! I see dust rising even to the heavens. I began to say to myself, "Are cattle approaching and raising the dust?" It was about a furlong's distance from me. And, lo! I see the dust rising more and more, so that I imagined that it was something sent from God. But the sun now shone out a little, and, lo! I see a mighty beast like a whale, and out of its mouth fiery locusts proceeded. But the size of that beast was about a hundred feet, and it had a head like an urn. I began to weep, and to call on the Lord to rescue me from it. Then I remembered the word which I had heard, "Doubt not, O Hermas." Clothed, therefore, my brethren, with faith in the Lord and remembering the great things which He had taught me, I boldly faced the beast. Now that beast came on with such noise and force, that it could itself have destroyed a city. I came near it, and the monstrous beast stretched itself out on the ground, and showed nothing but its tongue, and did not stir at all until I had passed by it. Now the beast had four colours on its head—black, then fiery and bloody, then golden, and lastly white.

Chapter 2

Now after I had passed by the wild beast, and had moved forward about thirty feet, lo! a virgin meets me, adorned as if she were proceeding from the bridal chamber, clothed entirely in white, and with white sandals, and veiled up to her forehead, and her head was covered by a hood. And she had white hair. I knew from my former visions that this was the Church, and I became more joyful. She saluted me, and said, "Hail, O man!" And I returned her salutation, and said, "Lady, hail!" And she answered, and said to me, "Has nothing crossed your path?" I say, "I was met by a beast of such a size that it could destroy peoples, but through the power of the Lord and His great mercy I escaped from it." "Well did you escape from it," says she, "because you cast your care on God, and opened your heart to the Lord, believing that you can be saved by no other than by His great and glorious name. On this account the Lord has sent His angel, who has rule over the beasts, and whose name is Thegri, and has shut up its mouth, so that it cannot tear you. You have escaped from great tribulation on account of your faith, and because you did not doubt in the presence of such a beast. Go, therefore, and tell the elect of the Lord His mighty deeds, and say to them that this beast is a type of the great tribulation that is coming. If then ye prepare yourselves, and repent with all your heart, and turn to the Lord, it will be possible for you to escape it, if your heart be pure and spotless, and ye spend the rest of the days of your life in serving the Lord blamelessly. Cast your cares upon the Lord, and He will direct them. Trust the Lord, ye who doubt, for He is all-powerful, and can turn His anger away from you, and send scourges on the doubters. Woe to those who hear these words, and despise them: better were it for them not to have been born."

190 ↝ THE APOSTOLIC FATHERS

I asked her about the four colours which the beast had on his head. And she answered, and said to me, "Again you are inquisitive in regard to such matters." "Yea, Lady," said I, "make known to me what they are." "Listen," said she: "the black is the world in which we dwell: but the fiery and bloody points out that the world must perish through blood and fire: but the golden part are you who have escaped from this world. For as gold is tested by fire, and thus becomes useful, so are you tested who dwell in it. Those, therefore, who continue steadfast, and are put through the fire, will be purified by means of it. For as gold casts away its dross, so also will ye cast away all sadness and straitness, and will be made pure so as to fit into the building of the tower. But the white part is the age that is to come, in which the elect of God will dwell, since those elected by God to eternal life will be spotless and pure. Wherefore cease not speaking these things into the ears of the saints. This then is the type of the great tribulation that is to come. If ye wish it, it will be nothing. Remember those things which were written down before." And saying this, she departed. But I saw not into what place she retired. There was a noise, however, and I turned round in alarm, thinking that that beast was coming.

Fifth Vision
Concerning the
Commandments

∾

AFTER I HAD BEEN praying at home, and had sat down on my couch, there entered a man of glorious aspect, dressed like a shepherd, with a white goat's skin, a wallet on his shoulders, and a rod in his hand, and saluted me. I returned his salutation. And straightway he sat down beside me, and said to me, "I have been sent by a most venerable angel to dwell with you the remaining days of your life." And I thought that he had come to tempt me, and I said to him, "Who are you? For I know him to whom I have been entrusted." He said to me, "Do you not know me?" "No," said I. "I," said he, "am that shepherd to whom you have been entrusted." And while he yet spake, his figure was changed; and then I knew that it was he to whom I had been entrusted. And straightway I became confused, and fear took hold of me, and I was overpowered with deep sorrow that I had answered him so wickedly and foolishly. But he answered, and said to me, "Do not be confounded, but receive strength from the commandments which I am going to give you. For I have been sent," said he, "to show you again all the things which you saw before, especially those of them which are useful to you. First of all, then, write down my commandments and similitudes, and you will write the other things as I shall show you. For this purpose," said he, "I command you to write down the commandments and similitudes first, that you may read them easily, and be able to keep them." Accordingly I wrote down the commandments and similitudes, exactly as he had ordered me. If then, when you have heard these, ye keep them and walk in them, and practice them with pure minds, you will receive from the Lord all that He has promised to you. But if, after you have heard them, ye do not repent, but continue to add to your sins, then shall ye receive from the Lord the opposite things. All these words did the shepherd, even the angel of repentance, command me to write.

THE PASTOR
SECOND BOOK—
COMMANDMENTS

First Commandment
On Faith in God

❦

FIRST OF ALL, BELIEVE that there is one God who created and finished all things, and made all things out of nothing. He alone is able to contain the whole, but Himself cannot be contained. Have faith therefore in Him, and fear Him; and fearing Him, exercise self-control. Keep these commands, and you will cast away from you all wickedness, and put on the strength of righteousness, and live to God, if you keep this commandment.

Second Commandment
On Avoiding
Evil-Speaking, and on
Giving Alms in Simplicity

❧

HE SAID TO ME, "Be simple and guileless, and you will be as the children who know not the wickedness that ruins the life of men. First, then, speak evil of no one, nor listen with pleasure to any one who speaks evil of another. But if you listen, you will partake of the sin of him who speaks evil, if you believe the slander which you hear; for believing it, you will also have something to say against your brother. Thus, then, will you be guilty of the sin of him who slanders. For slander is evil and an unsteady demon. It never abides in peace, but always remains in discord. Keep yourself from it, and you will always be at peace with all. Put on a holiness in which there is no wicked cause of offence, but all deeds that are equable and joyful. Practise goodness; and from the rewards of your labours, which God gives you, give to all the needy in simplicity, not hesitating as to whom you are to give or not to give. Give to all, for God wishes His gifts to be shared amongst all. They who receive, will render an account to God why and for what they have received. For the afflicted who receive will not be condemned, but they who receive on false pretences will suffer punishment. He, then, who gives is guiltless. For as he received from the Lord, so has he accomplished his service in simplicity, not hesitating as to whom he should give and to whom he should not give. This service, then, if accomplished in simplicity, is glorious with God. He, therefore, who thus ministers in simplicity, will live to God. Keep therefore these commandments, as I have given them to you, that your repentance and the repentance of your house may be found in simplicity, and your heart may be pure and stainless."

Third Commandment
On Avoiding Falsehood,
and on the
Repentance of Hermas
for His Dissimulation

∾

AGAIN HE SAID TO ME, "Love the truth, and let nothing but truth proceed from your mouth, that the spirit which God has placed in your flesh may be found truthful before all men; and the Lord, who dwelleth in you, will be glorified, because the Lord is truthful in every word, and in Him is no falsehood. They therefore who lie deny the Lord, and rob Him, not giving back to Him the deposit which they have received. For they received from Him a spirit free from falsehood. If they give him back this spirit untruthful, they pollute the commandment of the Lord, and become robbers." On hearing these words, I wept most violently. When he saw me weeping, he said to me, "Why do you weep?" And I said, "Because, sir, I know not if I can be saved." "Why?" said he. And I said, "Because, sir, I never spake a true word in my life, but have ever spoken cunningly to all, and have affirmed a lie for the truth to all; and no one ever contradicted me, but credit was given to my word. How then can I live, since I have acted thus?" And he said to me, "Your feelings are indeed right and sound, for you ought as a servant of God to have walked in truth, and not to have joined an evil conscience with the spirit of truth, nor to have caused sadness to the holy and true Spirit." And I said to him, "Never, sir, did I listen to these words with so much attention." And he said to me, "Now you hear them, and keep them, that even the falsehoods which you formerly told in your transactions may come to be believed through the truthfulness of your present statements. For even they can become worthy of credit. If you keep these precepts, and from this time forward you speak nothing but the truth, it will be possible for you to obtain life. And whosoever shall hear this commandment, and depart from that great wickedness falsehood, shall live to God.

Fourth Commandment
On Putting
One's Wife Away
for Adultery

∾

Chapter 1

"I CHARGE YOU," said he, "to guard your chastity, and let no thought enter your heart of another man's wife, or of fornication, or of similar iniquities; for by doing this you commit a great sin. But if you always remember your own wife, you will never sin. For if this thought enter your heart, then you will sin; and if, in like manner, you think other wicked thoughts, you commit sin. For this thought is great sin in a servant of God. But if any one commit this wicked deed, he works death for himself. Attend, therefore, and refrain from this thought; for where purity dwells, there iniquity ought not to enter the heart of a righteous man." I said to him, "Sir, permit me to ask you a few questions." "Say on," said he. And I said to him, "Sir, if any one has a wife who trusts in the Lord, and if he detect her in adultery, does the man sin if he continue to live with her?" And he said to me, "As long as he remains ignorant of her sin, the husband commits no transgression in living with her. But if the husband know that his wife has gone astray, and if the woman does not repent, but persists in her fornication, and yet the husband continues to live with her, he also is guilty of her crime, and a sharer in her adultery." And I said to him, "What then, sir, is the husband to do, if his wife continue in her vicious practices?" And he said, "The husband should put her away, and remain by himself. But if he put his wife away and marry another, he also commits adultery." And I said to him, "What if the woman put away should repent, and wish to return to her husband: shall she not be taken back by her husband?" And he said to me, "Assuredly. If the husband do not take her back, he sins, and brings a great sin upon himself; for he ought to take back the sinner who has repented. But not frequently. For there is but one repentance to the servants of God. In case, therefore, that the divorced wife may repent, the husband ought not to marry another, when his wife has been put away. In this matter man and woman are to be treated exactly in the same way. Moreover, adultery is committed not only by those who pollute their flesh, but by those who imitate the heathen in their actions. Wherefore if any one persists in such deeds, and repents not, withdraw from him, and cease to live with him, otherwise you are a sharer in his sin. Therefore has the injunction been laid on you, that you should remain by yourselves, both man and woman, for in such persons repentance can take place. But I do not," said he, "give opportunity for the doing of these deeds, but that he who has sinned may sin no more. But with regard to his previous transgressions, there is One who is able to provide a cure; for it is He, indeed, who has power over all."

Chapter 2

I asked him again, and said, "Since the Lord has vouchsafed to dwell always with me, bear with me while I utter a few words; for I understand nothing, and my heart has been hardened by my previous mode of life. Give me understanding, for I am exceedingly dull, and I understand absolutely nothing." And he answered and said unto me, "I am set over repentance, and I give understanding to all who repent. Do you not think," he said, "that it is great wisdom to repent? For repentance is great wisdom. For he who has sinned understands that he acted wickedly in the sight of the Lord, and remembers the actions he has done, and he repents, and no longer acts wickedly, but does good munificently, and humbles and torments his soul because he has sinned. You see, therefore, that repentance is great wisdom." And I said to him, "It is for this reason, sir, that I may know what works I should do, that I may live: for my sins are many and various." And he said to me, "You shall live if you keep my commandments, and walk in them; and whosoever shall hear and keep these commandments, shall live to God."

Chapter 3

And I said to him, "I should like to continue my questions." "Speak on," said he. And I said, "I heard, sir, some teachers maintain that there is no other repentance than that which takes place, when we descended into the water and received remission of our former sins." He said to me, "That was sound doctrine which you heard; for that is really the case. For he who has received remission of his sins ought not to sin any more, but to live in purity. Since, however, you inquire diligently into all things, I will point this also out to you, not as giving occasion for error to those who are to believe, or have lately believed, in the Lord. For those who have now believed, and those who are to believe, have not repentance for their sins; but they have remission of their previous sins. For to those who have been called before these days, the Lord has set repentance. For the Lord, knowing the heart, and foreknowing all things, knew the weakness of men and the manifold wiles of the devil, that he would inflict some evil on the servants of God, and would act wickedly towards them. The Lord, therefore, being merciful, has had mercy on the work of His hand, and has set repentance for them; and He has entrusted to me power over this repentance. And therefore I say to you, that if any one is tempted by the devil, and sins after that great and holy calling in which the Lord has called His people to everlasting life, he has opportunity to repent but once. But if he should sin frequently after this, and then repent, to such a man his repentance will be of no avail; for with difficulty will he live." And I said,

"Sir, I feel that life has come back to me in listening attentively to these commandments; for I know that I shall be saved, if in future I sin no more." And he said, "You will be saved, you and all who keep these commandments.

And again I asked him, saying, "Sir, since you have been so patient in listening to me, will you show me this also?" "Speak," said he. And I said, "If a wife or husband die, and the widower or widow marry, does he or she commit sin?" "There is no sin in marrying again," said he; "but if they remain unmarried, they gain greater honour and glory with the Lord; but if they marry, they do not sin. Guard, therefore, your chastity and purity, and you will live to God. What commandments I now give you, and what I am to give, keep from henceforth, yea, from the very day when you were entrusted to me, and I will dwell in your house. And your former sins will be forgiven, if you keep my commandments. And all shall be forgiven who keep these my commandments, and walk in this chastity."

Fifth Commandment
Of Sadness of Heart,
and of Patience

ର

Chapter 1

"**BE PATIENT,**" said he, "and of good understanding, and you will rule over every wicked work, and you will work all righteousness. For if you be patient, the Holy Spirit that dwells in you will be pure. He will not be darkened by any evil spirit, but, dwelling in a broad region, he will rejoice and be glad; and with the vessel in which he dwells he will serve God in gladness, having great peace within himself. But if any outburst of anger take place, forthwith the Holy Spirit, who is tender, is straitened, not having a pure place, and he seeks to depart. For he is choked by the vile spirit, and cannot attend on the Lord as he wishes, for anger pollutes him. For the Lord dwells in long-suffering, but the devil in anger. The two spirits, then, when dwelling in the same habitation, are at discord with each other, and are troublesome to that man in whom they dwell. For if an exceedingly small piece of wormwood be taken and put into a jar of honey, is not the honey entirely destroyed, and does not the exceedingly small piece of wormwood entirely take away the sweetness of the honey, so that it no longer affords any gratification to its owner, but has become bitter, and lost its use? But if the wormwood be not put into the honey, then the honey remains sweet, and is of use to its owner. You see, then, that patience is sweeter than honey, and useful to God, and the Lord dwells in it.

But anger is bitter and useless. Now, if anger be mingled with patience, the patience is polluted, and its prayer is not then useful to God." "I should like, sir," said I, "to know the power of anger, that I may guard myself against it." And he said, "If you do not guard yourself against it, you and your house lose all hope of salvation. Guard yourself, therefore, against it. For I am with you, and all will depart from it who repent with their whole heart. For I will be with them, and I will save them all. For all are justified by the most holy angel."

Chapter 2

"Hear now," said he, "how wicked is the action of anger, and in what way it overthrows the servants of God by its action, and turns them from righteousness. But it does not turn away those who are full of faith, nor does it act on them, for the power of the Lord is with them. It is the thoughtless and doubting that it turns away. For as soon as it sees such men standing steadfast, it throws itself into their hearts, and for nothing at all the man or woman becomes embittered on account of occurrences in their daily life, as for instance on account of their food, or some superfluous word that has been uttered, or on account of some friend, or some gift or debt, or some such senseless affair. For all these things are foolish and empty and unprofitable to the servants of God. But patience is great, and mighty, and strong, and calm in the midst of great enlargement, joyful, rejoicing, free from care, glorifying God at all times, having no bitterness in her, and abiding continually meek and quiet. Now this patience dwells with those who have complete faith. But anger is foolish, and fickle, and senseless. Now, of folly is begotten bitterness, and of bitterness anger, and of anger frenzy. This frenzy, the product of so many evils, ends in great and incurable sin. For when all these spirits dwell in one vessel in which the Holy Spirit also dwells, the vessel cannot contain them, but overflows. The tender Spirit, then, not being accustomed to dwell with the wicked spirit, nor with hardness, withdraws from such a man, and seeks to dwell with meekness and peacefulness. Then, when he withdraws from the man in whom he dwelt, the man is emptied of the righteous Spirit; and being henceforward filled with evil spirits, he is in a state of anarchy in every action, being dragged hither and thither by the evil spirits, and there is a complete darkness in his mind as to everything good. This, then, is what happens to all the angry. Wherefore do you depart from that most wicked spirit anger, and put on patience, and resist anger and bitterness, and you will be found in company with the purity which is loved by the Lord. Take care, then, that you neglect not by any chance this commandment: for if you obey this commandment, you will be able to keep all the other commandments which I am to give you. Be strong, then, in these commandments, and put on power, and let all put on power, as many as wish to walk in them."

Sixth Commandment
How to Recognise the Two Spirits Attendant on Each Man, and How to Distinguish the Suggestions of the One from Those of the Other

∾

Chapter 1

"I GAVE YOU," he said, "directions in the first commandment to attend to faith, and fear, and self-restraint." "Even so, sir," said I. And he said, "Now I wish to show you the powers of these, that you may know what power each possesses. For their powers are double, and have relation alike to the righteous and the unrighteous. Trust you, therefore, the righteous, but put no trust in the unrighteous. For the path of righteousness is straight, but that of unrighteousness is crooked. But walk in the straight and even way, and mind not the crooked. For the crooked path has no roads, but has many pathless places and stumbling-blocks in it, and it is rough and thorny. It is injurious to those who walk therein. But they who walk in the straight road walk evenly without stumbling, because it is neither rough nor thorny. You see, then, that it is better to walk in this road." "I wish to go by this road," said I. "You will go by it," said he; "and whoever turns to the Lord with all his heart will walk in it."

Chapter 2

"Hear now," said he, "in regard to faith. There are two angels with a man – one of righteousness, and the other of iniquity." And I said to him, "How, sir, am I to know the powers of these, for both angels dwell with me?" "Hear," said he, and "understand them. The angel of righteousness is gentle and modest, meek and peaceful. When, therefore, he ascends into your heart, forthwith he talks to you of righteousness, purity, chastity, contentment, and of every righteous deed and glorious virtue. When all these ascend into your heart, know that the angel of righteousness is with you. These are the deeds of the angel of righteousness. Trust him, then, and his works. Look now at the works of the angel of iniquity. First, he is wrathful, and bitter, and foolish, and his works are evil, and ruin the servants of God. When, then, he ascends into your heart, know him by his works." And I said to him, "How, sir, I shall perceive him, I do not know." "Hear and understand," said he. "When anger comes upon you, or harshness, know that he is in you; and you will know this to be the case also, when you are attacked by a longing after many transactions, and the richest delicacies, and drunken revels, and divers luxuries, and things improper, and by a hankering after women, and by overreaching, and pride, and blustering, and by whatever is like to these. When these ascend into your heart, know that the angel of iniquity is in you. Now that you know his works, depart from him, and in no respect trust him, because his deeds are evil, and unprofitable to the servants of God. These, then, are the actions of both angels. Understand them, and trust the angel of righteousness; but depart from the angel of iniquity, because his instruction is bad in every deed. For though a man be most faithful, and the thought of this angel ascend into his heart, that man or woman must sin. On the other hand, be a man or woman ever so bad, yet, if the works of the angel of righteousness ascend into his or her heart, he or she must do something good. You see, therefore, that it is good to follow the angel of righteousness, but to bid farewell to the angel of iniquity.

"This commandment exhibits the deeds of faith, that you may trust the works of the angel of righteousness, and doing them you may live to God. But believe the works of the angel of iniquity are hard. If you refuse to do them, you will live to God."

Seventh Commandment
On Fearing God, and
Not Fearing the Devil

∾

"FEAR," SAID HE, "the Lord, and keep His commandments. For if you keep the commandments of God, you will be powerful in every action, and every one of your actions will be incomparable. For, fearing the Lord, you will do all things well. This is the fear which you ought to have, that you may be saved. But fear not the devil; for, fearing the Lord, you will have dominion over the devil, for there is no power in him. But he in whom there is no power ought on no account to be an object of fear; but He in whom there is glorious power is truly to be feared. For every one that has power ought to be feared; but he who has not power is despised by all. Fear, therefore, the deeds of the devil, since they are wicked. For, fearing the Lord, you will not do these deeds, but will refrain from them. For fears are of two kinds: for if you do not wish to do that which is evil, fear the Lord, and you will not do it; but, again, if you wish to do that which is good, fear the Lord, and you will do it. Wherefore the fear of the Lord is strong, and great, and glorious. Fear, then, the Lord, and you will live to Him, and as many as fear Him and keep His commandments will live to God." "Why," said I, "sir, did you say in regard to those that keep His commandments, that they will live to God?" "Because," says he, "all creation fears the Lord, but all creation does not keep His commandments. They only who fear the Lord and keep His commandments have life with God; but as to those who keep not His commandments, there is no life in them."

Eighth Commandment
We Ought to Shun
That Which Is Evil, and
Do That Which Is Good

∽

"I told you," said he, "that the creatures of God are double, for restraint also is double; for in some cases restraint has to be exercised, in others there is no need for restraint." "Make known to me, sir," say I, "in what cases restraint has to be exercised and in what cases it has not." "Restrain yourself in regard to evil, and do it not; but exercise no restraint in regard to good, but do it. For if you exercise restraint in the doing of good, you will commit a great sin; but if you exercise restraint, so as not to do that which is evil, you are practicing great righteousness.

Restrain yourself, therefore, from all iniquity, and do that which is good." "What, sir," say I, "are the evil deeds from which we must restrain ourselves?" "Hear," says he: "from adultery and fornication, from unlawful revelling, from wicked luxury, from indulgence in many kinds of food and the extravagance of riches, and from boastfulness, and haughtiness, and insolence, and lies, and backbiting, and hypocrisy, from the remembrance of wrong, and from all slander. These are the deeds that are most wicked in the life of men. From all these deeds, therefore, the servant of God must restrain himself. For he who does not restrain himself from these, cannot live to God. Listen, then, to the deeds that accompany these." "Are there, sir," said I, "any other evil deeds?" "There are," says he; "and many of them, too, from which the servant of God must restrain himself—theft, lying, robbery, false witness, overreaching, wicked lust, deceit, vainglory, boastfulness, and all other vices like to these." "Do you not think that these are really wicked?" "Exceedingly wicked in the servants of God. From all of these the servant of God must restrain himself. Restrain yourself, then, from all these, that you may live to God, and you will be enrolled amongst those who restrain themselves in regard to these matters. These, then, are the things from which you must restrain yourself."

"But listen," says he, "to the things in regard to which you have not to exercise self-restraint, but which you ought to do. Restrain not yourself in regard to that which is good, but do it." "And tell me, sir," say I, "the nature of the good deeds, that I may walk in them and wait on them, so that doing them I can be saved." "Listen," says he, "to the good deeds which you ought to do, and in regard to which there is no self-restraint requisite. First of all there is faith, then fear of the Lord, love, concord, words of righteousness, truth, patience. Than these, nothing is better in the life of men. If any one attend to these, and restrain himself not from them, blessed is he in his life. Then there are the following attendant on these: helping widows, looking after orphans and the needy, rescuing the servants of God from necessities, the being hospitable—for in hospitality good-doing finds afield—never opposing any one, the being quiet, having fewer needs than all men, reverencing the aged, practicing righteousness, watching the brotherhood, bearing insolence, being long-suffering, encouraging those who are sick in soul, not casting those who have fallen into sin from the faith, but turning them back and restoring them to peace of mind, admonishing sinners, nor oppressing debtors and the needy, and if there are any other actions like these. Do these seem to you good?" says he. "For what, sir," say I, "is better than these?" "Walk in them," says he, "and restrain not yourself from them, and you will live to God. Keep, therefore, this commandment. If you do good, and restrain not yourself from it, you will live to God. And again, if you refuse to do evil, and restrain yourself from it you will live to God. And all will live to God who keep these commandments, and walk in them."

Ninth Commandment
Prayer Must Be Made to God
Without Ceasing, and With
Unwavering Confidence

∽

HE SAYS TO ME, "Put away doubting from you and do not hesitate to ask of the Lord, saying to yourself, 'How can I ask of the Lord and receive from Him, seeing I have sinned so much against Him?' Do not thus reason with yourself, but with all your heart turn to the Lord and ask of Him without doubting, and you will know the multitude of His tender mercies; that He will never leave you, but fulfil the request of your soul. For He is not like men, who remember evils done against them; but He Himself remembers not evils, and has compassion on His own creature. Cleanse, therefore, your heart from all the vanities of this world, and from the words already mentioned, and ask of the Lord and you will receive all, and in none of your requests will you be denied which you make to the Lord without doubting. But if you doubt in your heart, you will receive none of your requests. For those who doubt regarding God are double-souled, and obtain not one of their requests. But those who are perfect in faith ask everything, trusting in the Lord; and they obtain, because they ask nothing doubting, and not being double-souled. For every double-souled man, even if he repent, will with difficulty be saved. Cleanse your heart, therefore, from all doubt, and put on faith, because it is strong, and trust God that you will obtain from Him all that you ask. And if at any time, after you have asked of the Lord, you are slower in obtaining your request [than you expected], do not doubt because you have not soon obtained the request of your soul; for invariably it is on account of some temptation or some sin of which you are ignorant that you are slower in obtaining your request. Wherefore do not cease to make the request of your soul, and you will obtain it. But if you grow weary and waver in your request, blame yourself, and not Him who does not give to you. Consider this doubting state of mind, for it is wicked and senseless, and turns many away entirely from the faith, even though they be very strong. For this doubting is the daughter of the devil, and acts exceedingly wickedly to the servants of God. Despise, then, doubting, and gain the mastery over it in everything; clothing yourself with faith, which is strong and powerful. For faith promises all things, perfects all things; but doubt having no thorough faith in itself, fails in every work which it undertakes. You see, then," says he, "that, faith is from above—from the Lord—and has great power; but doubt is an earthly spirit, coming from the devil, and has no power. Serve, then, that which has power, namely faith, and keep away from doubt, which has no power, and you will live to God. And all will live to God whose minds have been set on these things."

Tenth Commandment
Of Grief, and Not Grieving
the Spirit of God
Which Is in Us

∾

Chapter 1

"**REMOVE FROM YOU,**" says he, "grief; for she is the sister of doubt and anger." "How, sir," say I, "is she the sister of these? for anger, doubt, and grief seem to be quite different from each other." "You are senseless, O man. Do you not perceive that grief is more wicked than all the spirits, and most terrible to the servants of God, and more than all other spirits destroys man and crushes out the Holy Spirit, and yet, on the other hand, she saves him?" "I am senseless, sir," say I, "and do not understand these parables. For how she can crush out, and on the other hand save, I do not perceive." "Listen," says he. "Those who have never searched for the truth, nor investigated the nature of the Divinity, but have simply believed, when they devote themselves to and become mixed up with business, and wealth, and heathen friendships, and many other actions of this world, do not perceive the parables of Divinity; for their minds are darkened by these actions, and they are corrupted and become dried up. Even as beautiful vines, when they are neglected, are withered up by thorns and divers plants, so men who have believed, and have afterwards fallen away into many of those actions above mentioned, go astray in their minds, and lose all understanding in regard to righteousness; for it they hear of righteousness, their minds are occupied with their business, and they give no heed at all. Those, on the other hand, who have the fear of God, and search after Godhead and truth, and have their hearts turned to the Lord, quickly perceive and understand what is said to them, because they have the fear of the Lord in them. For where the Lord dwells, there is much understanding. Cleave, then, to the Lord, and you will understand and perceive all things."

Chapter 2

"Hear, then," says he, "foolish man, how grief crushes out the Holy Spirit, and on the other hand saves. When the doubting man attempts any deed, and fails in it on account of his doubt, this grief enters into the man, and grieves the Holy Spirit, and crushes him out. Then, on the other hand, when anger attaches itself to a man in regard to any matter, and he is embittered, then grief enters into the heart of the man who was irritated, and he is grieved at the deed which he did, and repents that he has wrought a wicked deed. This grief, then, appears to be accompanied by salvation, because the man, after having done a wicked deed, repented. Both actions grieve the Spirit: doubt, because it did not accomplish its object; and anger grieves the Spirit, because it did what was wicked. Both these are grievous to the Holy Spirit— doubt and anger. Wherefore remove grief from you, and crush not the Holy Spirit which dwells in you, lest he entreat God against you, and he withdraw from you. For the Spirit of God which has been granted to us to dwell in this body does not endure grief nor straitness. Wherefore put on cheerfulness, which always is agreeable and acceptable to God, and rejoice in it. For every cheerful man does what is good, and minds what is good, and despises grief; but the sorrowful man always acts wickedly. First, he acts wickedly because he grieves the Holy Spirit, which was given to man a cheerful Spirit. Secondly, Grieving the Holy Spirit, he works iniquity, neither entreating the Lord nor confessing to Him. For the entreaty of the sorrowful man has no power to ascend to the altar of God." "Why," say I, "does not the entreaty of the grieved man ascend to the altar?" "Because," says he, "grief sits in his heart. Grief, then, mingled with his entreaty, does not permit the entreaty to ascend pure to the altar of God. For as vinegar and wine, when mixed in the same vessel, do not give the same pleasure [as wine alone gives], so grief mixed with the Holy Spirit does not produce the same entreaty [as would be produced by the Holy Spirit alone]. Cleanse yourself from this wicked grief, and you will live to God; and all will live to God who drive away grief from them, and put on all cheerfulness."

Eleventh Commandment
The Spirit and Prophets to Be Tried by Their Works; also of the Two Kinds of Spirit

∾

HE POINTED OUT to me some men sitting on a seat, and one man sitting on a chair. And he says to me, "Do you see the persons sitting on the seat?" "I do, sir," said I. "These," says he, "are the faithful, and he who sits on the chair is a false prophet, ruining the minds of the servants of God. It is the doubters, not the faithful, that he ruins. These doubters then go to him as to a soothsayer, and inquire of him what will happen to them; and he, the false prophet, not having the power of a Divine Spirit in him, answers them according to their inquiries, and according to their wicked desires, and fills their souls with expectations, according to their own wishes. For being himself empty, he gives empty answers to empty inquirers; for every answer is made to the emptiness of man. Some true words he does occasionally utter; for the devil fills him with his own spirit, in the hope that he may be able to overcome some of the righteous. As many, then, as are strong in the faith of the Lord, and are clothed with truth, have no connection with such spirits, but keep away from them; but as many as are of doubtful minds and frequently repent, betake themselves to soothsaying, even as the heathen, and bring greater sin upon themselves by their idolatry. For he who inquires of a false prophet in regard to any action is an idolater, and devoid of the truth, and foolish. For no spirit given by God requires to be asked; but such a spirit having the power of Divinity speaks all things of itself, for it proceeds from above from the power of the Divine Spirit. But the spirit which is asked and speaks according to the desires of men is earthly, light, and powerless, and it is altogether silent if it is not questioned." "How then, sir," say I, "will a man know which of them is the prophet, and which the false prophet?" "I will tell you," says he, "about both the prophets, and then you can try the true and the false prophet according to my directions. Try the man who has the Divine Spirit by his life. First, he who has the Divine Spirit proceeding from above is meek, and peaceable, and humble, and refrains from all iniquity and the vain desire of this world, and contents himself with fewer wants than those of other men, and when asked he makes no reply; nor does he speak privately, nor when man wishes the spirit to speak does the Holy Spirit speak, but it speaks only when God wishes it to speak. When, then, a man having the Divine Spirit comes into an assembly of righteous men who have faith in the Divine Spirit, and this assembly of men offers up prayer to God, then the angel of the prophetic Spirit, who is destined for him, fills the man; and the man being filled with the Holy Spirit, speaks to the multitude as the Lord wishes. Thus, then, will the Spirit of Divinity become manifest. Whatever power therefore comes from the Spirit of Divinity belongs to the Lord. Hear, then," says he, "in regard to the spirit which is earthly, and empty, and powerless, and foolish. First, the man who seems to have the Spirit exalts himself, and wishes to have the first seat, and is bold, and impudent, and talkative, and lives in the midst of many luxuries and many other delusions, and takes rewards for his prophecy; and if he does not receive rewards, he does not prophesy. Can, then, the Divine Spirit take rewards and prophesy? It is not possible that the prophet of God should do this, but prophets of this character are possessed by an earthly spirit. Then it never approaches an assembly of righteous men, but shuns them. And it associates with doubters and the vain, and prophesies to them in a corner, and deceives them, speaking to them, according to their desires, mere empty words: for they are empty to whom it gives its answers. For the empty vessel, when placed along with the empty, is not crushed, but they correspond to each other. When, therefore, it comes into an assembly of righteous men who have a Spirit of Divinity, and they offer up prayer, that man is made empty, and the earthly spirit flees from him through fear, and that man is made dumb, and is entirely crushed, being unable to speak. For if you pack closely a storehouse with wine or oil, and put an empty jar in the midst of the vessels of wine or oil, you will find that jar empty as when you placed it, if you should wish to clear the storehouse. So also the empty prophets, when they come to the spirits of the righteous, are found [on leaving] to be such as they were when they came. This, then, is the mode of life of both prophets. Try by his deeds and his life the man who says that he is inspired. But as for you, trust the Spirit which comes from God, and has power; but the spirit which is earthly and empty trust not at all, for there is no power in it: it comes from the devil. Hear, then, the parable which I am to tell you. Take a stone, and throw it to the sky, and see if you can touch it. Or again, take a squirt of water and squirt into the sky, and see if you can penetrate the sky." "How, sir," say I, "can these things take place? for both of them are impossible." "As these things," says he, "are impossible, so also are the earthly spirits powerless and pithless. But look, on the other hand, at the power which comes from above. Hail is of the size of a very small grain, yet when it falls on a man's head how much annoyance it gives him! Or, again, take the drop which falls from a pitcher to the ground, and yet it hollows a stone. You see, then, that the smallest things coming from above have great power when they fall upon the earth. Thus also is the Divine Spirit, which comes from above, powerful. Trust, then, that Spirit, but have nothing to do with the other."

Twelfth Commandment
On the Twofold Desire.
The Commandments of God
Can Be Kept, and Believers
Ought Not to Fear the Devil

∾

Chapter 1

HE SAYS TO ME, "Put away from you all wicked desire, and clothe yourself with good and chaste desire; for clothed with this desire you will hate wicked desire, and will rein yourself in even as you wish. For wicked desire is wild, and is with difficulty tamed. For it is terrible, and consumes men exceedingly by its wildness. Especially is the servant of God terribly consumed by it, if he falls into it and is devoid of understanding. Moreover, it consumes all such as have not on them the garment of good desire, but are entangled and mixed up with this world. These it delivers up to death." "What then, sir," say I, "are the deeds of wicked desire which deliver men over to death? Make them known to me, and I will refrain from them." "Listen, then, to the works in which evil desire slays the servants of God."

Chapter 2

"Foremost of all is the desire after another's wife or husband, and after extravagance, and many useless dainties and drinks, and many other foolish luxuries; for all luxury is foolish and empty in the servants of God. These, then, are the evil desires which slay the servants of God. For this evil desire is the daughter of the devil. You must refrain from evil desires, that by refraining ye may live to God. But as many as are mastered by them, and do not resist them, will perish at last, for these desires are fatal. Put you on, then, the desire of righteousness; and arming yourself with the fear of the Lord, resist them. For the fear of the Lord dwells in good desire. But if evil desire see you armed with the fear of God, and resisting it, it will flee far from you, and it will no longer appear to you, for it fears your armour. Go, then, garlanded with the crown which you have gained for victory over it, to the desire of righteousness, and, delivering up to it the prize which you have received, serve it even as it wishes. If you serve good desire, and be subject to it, you will gain the mastery over evil desire, and make it subject to you even as you wish."

Chapter 3

"I should like to know," say I, "in what way I ought to serve good desire." "Hear," says he: "You will practice righteousness and virtue, truth and the fear of the Lord, faith and meekness, and whatsoever excellences are like to these. Practising these, you will be a well-pleasing servant of God, and you will live to Him;

and every one who shall serve good desire, shall live to God."

He concluded the twelve commandments, and said to me, "You have now these commandments. Walk in them, and exhort your hearers that their repentance may be pure during the remainder of their life. Fulfil carefully this ministry which I now entrust to you, and you will accomplish much. For you will find favour among those who are to repent and they will give heed to your words; for I will be with you, and will compel them to obey you." I say to him, "Sir, these commandments are great, and good, and glorious, and fitted to gladden the heart of the man who can perform them. But I do not know if these commandments can be kept by man, because they are exceeding hard." He answered and said to me, "If you lay it down as certain that they can be kept, then you will easily keep them, and they will not be hard. But if you come to imagine that they cannot be kept by man, then you will not keep them. Now I say to you, If you do not keep them, but neglect them, you will not be saved, nor your children, nor your house, since you have already determined for yourself that these commandments cannot be kept by man."

Chapter 4

These things he said to me in tones of the deepest anger, so that I was confounded and exceedingly afraid of him, for his figure was altered so that a man could not endure his anger. But seeing me altogether agitated and confused, he began to speak to me in more gentle tones; and he said: "O fool, senseless and doubting, do you not perceive how great is the glory of God, and how strong and marvellous, in that He created the world for the sake of man, and subjected all creation to him, and gave him power to rule over everything under heaven? If, then, man is lord of the creatures of God, and rules over all, is he not able to be lord also of these commandments? For," says he, "the man who has the Lord in his heart can also be lord of all, and of every one of these commandments. But to those who have the Lord only on their lips, but their hearts hardened, and who are far from the Lord, the commandments are hard and difficult. Put, therefore, ye who are empty and fickle in your faith, the Lord in your heart, and ye will know that there is nothing easier or sweeter, or more manageable, than these commandments. Return, ye who walk in the commandments of the devil, in hard, and bitter, and wild licentiousness, and fear not the devil; for there is no power in him against you, for I will be with you, the angel of repentance, who am lord over him. The devil has fear only, but his fear has no strength. Fear him not, then, and he will flee from you."

Chapter 5

I say to him, "Sir, listen to me for a moment." "Say what you wish," says he. "Man, sir," say I, "is eager to keep the commandments of God, and there is no one who does not ask of the Lord that strength may be given him for these commandments, and that he may be subject to them; but the devil is hard, and holds sway over them." "He cannot," says he, "hold sway over the servants of God, who with all their heart place their hopes in Him. The devil can wrestle against these, overthrow them he cannot. If, then, ye resist him, he will be conquered, and flee in disgrace from you. As many, therefore," says he, "as are empty, fear the devil, as possessing power. When a man has filled very suitable jars with good wine, and a few among those jars are left empty, then he comes to the jars, and does not look at the full jars, for he knows that they are full; but he looks at the empty, being afraid lest they have become sour. For empty jars quickly become sour, and the goodness of the wine is gone. So also the devil goes to all the servants of God to try them. As many, then, as are full in the faith, resist him strongly, and he withdraws from them, having no way by which he might enter them. He goes, then, to the empty, and finding a way of entrance, into them, he produces in them whatever he wishes, and they become his servants."

Chapter 6

"But I, the angel of repentance, say to you, Fear not the devil; for I was sent," says he, "to be with you who repent with all your heart, and to make you strong in faith. Trust God, then, ye who on account of your sins have despaired of life, and who add to your sins and weigh down your life; for if ye return to the Lord with all your heart, and practice righteousness the rest of your days, and serve Him according to His will, He will heal your former sins, and you will have power to hold sway over the works of the devil. But as to the threats of the devil, fear them not at all, for he is powerless as the sinews of a dead man. Give ear to me, then, and fear Him who has all power, both to save and destroy, and keep His commandments, and ye will live to God." I say to him, "Sir, I am now made strong in all the ordinances of the Lord, because you are with me; and I know that you will crush all the power of the devil, and we shall have rule over him, and shall prevail against all his works. And I hope, sir, to be able to keep all these commandments which you have enjoined upon me, the Lord strengthening me." "You will keep them," says he, "if your heart be pure towards the Lord; and all will keep them who cleanse their hearts from the vain desires of this world, and they will live to God."

THE PASTOR
THIRD BOOK—
SIMILITUDES

.

First Similitude
As in This World
We Have No Abiding
City, We Ought to
Seek One to Come

∞

HE SAYS TO ME, "You know that you who are the servants of God dwell in a strange land; for your city is far away from this one. If, then," he continues, "you know your city in which you are to dwell, why do ye here provide lands, and make expensive preparations, and accumulate dwellings and useless buildings? He who makes such preparations for this city cannot return again to his own. Oh foolish, and unstable, and miserable man! Dost thou not understand that all these things belong to another, and are under the power of another? for the lord of this city will say, 'I do not wish thee to dwell in my city; but depart from this city, because thou obeyest not my laws.' Thou, therefore, although having fields and houses, and many other things, when cast out by him, what wilt thou do with thy land, and house, and other possessions which thou hast gathered to thyself? For the lord of this country justly says to thee, 'Either obey my laws or depart from my dominion.' What, then, dost thou intend to do, having a law in thine own city, on account of thy lands, and the rest of thy possessions? Thou shalt altogether deny thy law, and walk according to the law of this city. See lest it be to thy hurt to deny thy law; for if thou shalt desire to return to thy city, thou wilt not be received, because thou hast denied the law of thy city, but be excluded from it. Have a care, therefore: as one living in a foreign land, make no further preparations for thyself than such merely as may be sufficient; and be ready, when the master of this city shall come to cast thee out for disobeying his law, to leave his city, and to depart to thine own, and to obey thine own law without being exposed to annoyance, but in great joy. Have a care, then, ye who serve the Lord, and have Him in your heart, that ye work the works of God, remembering His commandments and promises which He promised, and believe that He will bring them to pass if His commandments be observed. Instead of lands, therefore, buy afflicted souls, according as each one is able, and visit widows and orphans, and do not overlook them; and spend your wealth and all your preparations, which ye received from the Lord, upon such lands and houses. For to this end did the Master make you rich, that you might perform these services unto Him; and it is much better to purchase such lands, and possessions, and houses, as you will find in your own city, when you come to reside in it. This is a noble and sacred expenditure, attended neither with sorrow nor fear, but with joy. Do not practice the expenditure of the heathen, for it is injurious to you who are the servants of God; but practice an expenditure of your own, in which ye can rejoice; and do not corrupt nor touch what is another's nor covet it, for it is an evil thing to covet the goods of other men; but work thine own work, and thou wilt be saved."

Second Similitude
As the Vine Is Supported
by the Elm, So Is the
Rich Man Helped
by the Prayer of the Poor

∾

AS I WAS WALKING in the field, and observing an elm and vine, and determining in my own mind respecting them and their fruits, the Shepherd appears to me, and says, "What is it that you are thinking about the elm and vine?" "I am considering," I reply, "that they become each other exceedingly well." "These two trees," he continues, "are intended as an example for the servants of God." "I would like to know," said I, "the example which these trees you say, are intended to teach." "Do you see," he says, "the elm and the vine?" "I see them sir," I replied. "This vine," he continued, "produces fruit, and the elm is an unfruitful tree; but unless the vine be trained upon the elm, it cannot bear much fruit when extended at length upon the ground; and the fruit which it does bear is rotten, because the plant is not suspended upon the elm. When, therefore, the vine is cast upon the elm, it yields fruit both from itself and from the elm. You see, moreover, that the elm also produces much fruit, not less than the vine, but even more; because," he continued, "the vine, when suspended upon the elm, yields much fruit, and good; but when thrown upon the ground, what it produces is small and rotten. This similitude, therefore, is for the servants of God—for the poor man and for the rich." "How so, sir?" said I; "explain the matter to me." "Listen," he said: "The rich man has much wealth, but is poor in matters relating to the Lord, because he is distracted about his riches; and he offers very few confessions and intercessions to the Lord, and those which he does offer are small and weak, and have no power above. But when the rich man refreshes the poor, and assists him in his necessities, believing that what he does to the poor man will be able to find its reward with God—because the poor man is rich in intercession and confession, and his intercession has great power with God—then the rich man helps the poor in all things without hesitation; and the poor man, being helped by the rich, intercedes for him, giving thanks to God for him who bestows gifts upon him. And he still continues to interest himself zealously for the poor man, that his wants may be constantly supplied. For he knows that the intercession of the poor man is acceptable and influential with God. Both, accordingly, accomplish their work. The poor man makes intercession; a work in which he is rich, which he received from the Lord, and with which he recompenses the master who helps him. And the rich man, in like manner, unhesitatingly bestows upon the poor man the riches which he received from the Lord. And this is a great work, and acceptable before God, because he understands the object of his wealth, and has given to the poor of the gifts of the Lord, and rightly discharged his service to Him. Among men, however, the elm appears not to produce fruit, and they do not know nor understand that if a drought come, the elm, which contains water, nourishes the vine; and the vine, having an unfailing supply of water, yields double fruit both for itself and for the elm. So also poor men interceding with the Lord on behalf of the rich, increase their riches; and the rich, again, aiding the poor in their necessities, satisfy their souls. Both, therefore, are partners in the righteous work. He who does these things shall not be deserted by God, but shall be enrolled in the books of the living. Blessed are they who have riches, and who understand that they are from the Lord. [For they who are of that mind will be able to do some good.

Third Similitude
As in Winter
Green Trees Cannot be
Distinguished from Withered,
So in This World Neither
Can the Just from the Unjust

∾

HE SHOWED ME many trees having no leaves, but withered, as it seemed to me; for all were alike. And he said to me, "Do you see those trees?" "I see, sir," I replied, "that all are alike, and withered." He answered me, and said, "These trees which you see are those who dwell in this world." "Why, then, sir," I said, "are they withered, as it were, and alike?" "Because," he said, "neither are the righteous manifest in this life, nor sinners, but they are alike; for this life is a winter to the righteous, and they do not manifest themselves, because they dwell with sinners: for as in winter trees that have cast their leaves are alike, and it is not seen which are dead and which are living, so in this world neither do the righteous show themselves, nor sinners, but all are alike one to another."

Fourth Similitude
As in Summer Living Trees Are Distinguished from Withered by Fruit and Living Leaves, So in the World to Come the Just Differ From the Unjust in Happinesss

HE SHOWED ME again many trees, some budding, and others withered. And he said to me, "Do you see these trees?" "I see, sir," I replied, "some putting forth buds, and others withered." "Those,' he said, "which are budding are the righteous who are to live in the world to come; for the coming world is the summer of the righteous, but the winter of sinners. When, therefore, the mercy of the Lord shines forth, then shall they be made manifest who are the servants of God, and all men shall be made manifest. For as in summer the fruits of each individual tree appear, and it is ascertained of what sort they are, so also the fruits of the righteous shall be manifest, and all who have been fruitful in that world shall be made known. But the heathen and sinners, like the withered trees which you saw, will be found to be those who have been withered and unfruitful in that world, and shall be burnt as wood, and [so] made manifest, because their actions were evil during their lives. For the sinners shall be consumed because they sinned and did not repent, and the heathen shall be burned because they knew not Him who created them. Do you therefore bear fruit, that in that summer your fruit may be known. And refrain from much business, and you will never sin: for they who are occupied with much business commit also many sins, being distracted about their affairs, and not at all serving their Lord. "How, then," he continued, "can such a one ask and obtain anything from the Lord, if he serve Him not? They who serve Him shall obtain their requests, but they who serve Him not shall receive nothing. And in the performance even of a single action a man can serve the Lord; for his mind will not be perverted from the Lord, but he will serve Him, having a pure mind. If, therefore, you do these things, you shall be able to bear fruit for the life to come. And every one who will do these things shall bear fruit."

Fifth Similitude
Of True Fasting
and Its Reward:
Also of Purity of Body

∾

Chapter 1

WHILE FASTING AND SITTING on a certain mountain, and giving thanks to the Lord for all His dealings with me, I see the Shepherd sitting down beside me, and saying, "Why have you come hither [so] early in the morning?" "Because, sir," I answered, "I have a station." "What is a station?" he asked. "I am fasting, sir," I replied. "What is this fasting," he continued, "which you are observing?" "As I have been accustomed, sir," I reply, "so I fast." "You do not know," he says, "how to fast unto the Lord: this useless fasting which you observe to HIM is of no value." "Why, sir," I answered, "do you say this? "I say to you," he continued, "that the fasting which you think you observe is not a fasting. But I will teach you what is a full and acceptable fasting to the Lord. Listen," he continued: "God does not desire such an empty fasting. For fasting to God in this way you will do nothing for a righteous life; but offer to God a fasting of the following kind: Do no evil in your life, and serve the Lord with a pure heart: keep His commandments, walking in His precepts, and let no evil desire arise in your heart; and believe in God. If you do these things, and fear Him, and abstain from every evil thing, you will live unto God; and if you do these things, you will keep a great fast, and one acceptable before God."

Chapter 2

"Hear the similitude which I am about to narrate to you relative to fasting. A certain man had a field and many slaves, and he planted a certain part of the field with a vineyard, and selecting a faithful and beloved and much valued slave, he called him to him, and said, 'Take this vineyard which I have planted, and stake it until I come, and do nothing else to the vineyard; and attend to this order of mine, and you shall receive your freedom from me.' And the master of the slave departed to a foreign country. And when he was gone, the slave took and staked the vineyard; and when he had finished the staking of the vines, he saw that the vineyard was full of weeds. He then reflected, saying, 'I have kept this order of my master: I will dig up the rest of this vineyard, and it will be more beautiful when dug up; and being free of weeds, it will yield more fruit, not being choked by them.' He took, therefore, and dug up the vineyard, and rooted out all the weeds that were in it. And that vineyard became very beautiful and fruitful, having no weeds to choke it. And after a certain time the master of the slave and of the field returned, and entered into the vineyard. And seeing that the vines were suitably supported on stakes, and the ground, moreover, dug up, and all the weeds rooted out, and the vines fruitful, he was greatly pleased with the work of his slave. And calling his beloved son who was his heir, and his friends who were his councillors, he told them what orders he had given his slave, and what he had found performed. And they rejoiced along with the slave at the testimony which his master bore to him. And he said to them, 'I promised this slave freedom if he obeyed the command which I gave him; and he has kept my command, and done besides a good work to the vineyard, and has pleased me exceedingly. In return, therefore, for the work which he has done, I wish to make him co-heir with my son, because, having good thoughts, he did not neglect them, but carried them out.' With this resolution of the master his son and friends were well pleased, viz., that the slave should be co-heir with the son. After a few days the master made a feast, and sent to his slave many dishes from his table. And the slave receiving the dishes that were sent him from his master, took of them what was sufficient for himself, and distributed the rest among his fellow-slaves. And his fellow-slaves rejoiced to receive the dishes, and began to pray for him, that he might find still greater favour with his master for having so treated them. His master heard all these things that were done, and was again greatly pleased with his conduct. And the master again calling together his friends and his son, reported to them the slave's proceeding with regard to the dishes which he had sent him. And they were still more satisfied that the slave should become co-heir with his son."

Chapter 3

I said to him, "Sir, I do not see the meaning of these similitudes, nor am I able to comprehend them, unless you explain them to me." "I will explain them all to you," he said, "and whatever I shall mention in the course of our conversations I will show you. [Keep the commandments of the Lord, and you will be approved, and inscribed amongst the number of those who observe His commands.] And if you do any good beyond what is commanded by God, you will gain for yourself more abundant glory, and will be more honoured by God than you would otherwise be. If, therefore, in keeping the commandments of God, you do, in addition, these services, you will have joy if you observe them according to my command." I said to him, "Sir, whatsoever you enjoin upon me I will observe, for I know that you are with me." "I will be with you," he replied, "because you have such a desire for doing good; and I will be with all those," he added, "who have such a desire. This fasting," he continued, "is very good, provided the commandments of the Lord be observed. Thus, then, shall you observe the fasting which you intend to keep. First of all, be on your guard against every evil word, and every evil desire, and purify your heart from all the vanities of this world. If you guard against these things, your fasting will be perfect. And you will do also as follows. Having fulfilled what is written, in the day on which you fast you will taste nothing but bread and water; and having reckoned up the price of the dishes of that day which you intended to have eaten, you will give it to a widow, or an orphan, or to some person in want, and thus you will exhibit humility of mind, so that he who has received benefit from your humility may fill his own soul, and pray for you to the Lord. If you observe fasting, as I have commanded you, your sacrifice will be acceptable to God, and this fasting will be written down; and the service thus performed is noble, and sacred, and acceptable to the Lord. These things, therefore, shall you thus observe with your children, and all your house, and in observing them you will be blessed; and as many as hear these words and observe them shall be blessed; and whatsoever they ask of the Lord they shall receive."

Chapter 4

I prayed him much that he would explain to me the similitude of the field, and of the master of the vineyard, and of the slave who staked the vineyard, and of the sakes, and of the weeds that were plucked out of the vineyard, and of the son, and of the friends who were fellow-councillors, for I knew that all these things were a kind of parable. And he answered me, and said, "You are exceedingly persistent with your questions. You ought not," he continued, "to ask any questions at all; for if it is needful to explain anything, it will be made known to you." I said to him,

"Sir, whatsoever you show me, and do not explain, I shall have seen to no purpose, not understanding its meaning. In like manner, also, if you speak parables to me, and do not unfold them, I shall have heard your words in vain." And he answered me again, saying, "Every one who is the servant of God, and has his Lord in his heart, asks of Him understanding, and receives it, and opens up every parable; and the words of the Lord become known to him which are spoken in parables. But those who are weak and slothful in prayer, hesitate to ask anything from the Lord; but the Lord is full of compassion, and gives without fail to all who ask Him. But you, having been strengthened by the holy Angel, and having obtained from Him such intercession, and not being slothful, why do not you ask of the Lord understanding, and receive it from Him?" I said to him, "Sir, having you with me, I am necessitated to ask questions of you, for you show me all things, and converse with me; but if I were to see or hear these things without you, I would then ask the Lord to explain them."

Chapter 5

"I said to you a little ago," he answered, "that you were cunning and obstinate in asking explanations of the parables; but since you are so persistent, I shall unfold to you the meaning of the similitudes of the field, and of all the others that follow, that you may make them known to every one. Hear now," he said, "and understand them. The field is this world; and the Lord of the field is He who created, and perfected, and strengthened all things;

[and the son is the Holy Spirit;] and the slave is the Son of God; and the vines are this people, whom He Himself planted; and the stakes are the holy angels of the Lord, who keep His people together; and the weeds that were plucked out of the vineyard are the iniquities of God's servants; and the dishes which He sent Him from His table are the commandments which He gave His people through His Son; and the friends and fellow-councillors are the holy angels who were first created; and the Master's absence from home is the time that remains until His appearing." I said to him, "Sir, all these are great, and marvellous, and glorious things. Could I, therefore," I continued, "understand them? No, nor could any other man, even if exceedingly wise. Moreover," I added, "explain to me what I am about to ask you." "Say what you wish," he replied. "Why, sir," I asked, "is the Son of God in the parable in the form of a slave?"

Chapter 6

"Hear," he answered: "the Son of God is not in the form of a slave, but in great power and might." "How so, sir?" I said; "I do not understand." "Because," he answered, "God planted the vineyard, that is to say, He created the people, and gave them to His Son; and the Son appointed His angels over them to keep them; and He Himself purged away their sins, having suffered many trials and undergone many labours, for no one is able to dig without labour and toil. He Himself, then, having purged away the sins of the people, showed them the paths of life by giving them the law which He received from His Father. [You see," he said, "that He is the Lord of the people, having received all authority from His Father.] And why the Lord took His Son as councillor, and the glorious angels, regarding the heirship of the slave, listen. The holy, pre-existent Spirit, that created every creature, God made to dwell in flesh, which He chose. This flesh, accordingly, in which the Holy Spirit dwelt, was nobly subject to that Spirit, walking religiously and chastely, in no respect defiling the Spirit; and accordingly, after living excellently and purely, and after laboring and cooperating with the Spirit, and having in everything acted vigorously and courageously along with the Holy Spirit, He assumed it as a partner with it. For this conduct of the flesh pleased Him, because it was not defiled on the earth while having the Holy Spirit. He took, therefore, as fellow-councillors His Son and the glorious angels, in order that this flesh, which had been subject to the body without a fault, might have some place of tabernacle, and that it might not appear that the reward [of its servitude had been lost], for the flesh that has been found without spot or defilement, in which the Holy Spirit dwelt, [will receive a reward]. You have now the explanation of this parable also."

Chapter 7

"I rejoice, sir," I said, "to hear this explanation." "Hear," again he replied: "Keep this flesh pure and stainless, that the Spirit which inhabits it may bear witness to it, and your flesh may be justified. See that the thought never arise in your mind that this flesh of yours is corruptible, and you misuse it by any act of defilement. If you defile your flesh, you will also defile the Holy Spirit; and if you defile your flesh [and spirit], you will not live." "And if any one, sir," I said, "has been hitherto ignorant, before he heard these words, how can such a man be saved who has defiled his flesh?" "Respecting former sins of ignorance," he said, "God alone is able to heal them, for to Him belongs all power. [But be on your guard now, and the all-powerful and compassionate God will heal former transgressions], if for the time to come you defile not your body nor your spirit; for both are common, and cannot be defiled, the one without the other: keep both therefore pure, and you will live unto God."

Sixth Similitude
Of the Two Classes of
Voluptuous Men, and of Their
Death, Falling Away, and the
Duration of Their Punishment

∾

Chapter 1

SITTING IN MY HOUSE, and glorifying the Lord for all that I had
seen, and reflecting on the commandments, that they are excellent, and powerful, and glorious, and able to save a man's soul, I
said within myself, "I shall be blessed if I walk in these commandments, and every one who walks in them will be blessed."
While I was saying these words to myself, I suddenly see him sitting beside me, and hear him thus speak: "Why are you in doubt
about the commandments which I gave you? They are excellent:
have no doubt about them at all, but put on faith in the Lord, and
you will walk in them, for I will strengthen you in them. These
commandments are beneficial to those who intend to repent: for
if they do not walk in them, their repentance is in vain. You,
therefore, who repent cast away the wickedness of this world

which wears you out; and by putting on all the virtues of a holy life, you will be able to keep these commandments, and will no longer add to the number of your sins. Walk, therefore, in these commandments of mine, and you will live unto God. All these things have been spoken to you by me." And after he had uttered these words, he said to me, "Let us go into the fields, and I will show you the shepherds of the flocks." "Let us go, sir," I replied. And we came to a certain plain, and he showed me a young man, a shepherd, clothed in a suit of garments of a yellow colour: and he was herding very many sheep, and these sheep were feeding luxuriously, as it were, and riotously, and merrily skipping hither and thither. The shepherd himself was merry, because of his flock; and the appearance of the shepherd was joyous, and he was running about amongst his flock. [And other sheep I saw rioting and luxuriating in one place, but not, however, leaping about.]

Chapter 2

And he said to me, "Do you see this shepherd?" "I see him, sir," I said. "This," he answered, "is the angel of luxury and deceit: he wears out the souls of the servants of God, and perverts them from the truth, deceiving them with wicked desires, through which they will perish; for they forget the commandments of the living God, and walk in deceits and empty luxuries; and they are ruined by the angel, some being brought to death, others to corruption." I said to him, "Sir, I do not know the meaning of these words, 'to death, and to corruption.'" "Listen," he said. "The sheep which you saw merry and leaping about, are those which have torn themselves away from God for ever, and have delivered themselves over to luxuries and deceits [of this world. Among them there is no return to life through repentance, because they have added to their other sins, and blasphemed the name of the Lord. Such men therefore, are appointed unto death. And the sheep which you saw not leaping, but feeding in one place, are they who have delivered themselves over to luxury and deceit], but have committed no blasphemy against the Lord. These have been perverted from the truth: among them there is the hope of repentance, by which it is possible to live. Corruption, then, has a hope of a kind of renewal, but death has everlasting ruin." Again I went forward a little way, and he showed me a tall shepherd, somewhat savage in his appearance, clothed in a white goatskin, and having a wallet on his shoulders, and a very hard staff with branches, and a large whip. And he had a very sour look, so that I was afraid of him, so forbidding was his aspect. This shepherd, accordingly, was receiving the sheep from the young shepherd, those, viz., that were rioting and luxuriating, but not leaping; and he cast them into a precipitous place, full of thistles and thorns, so that it was impossible to extricate the sheep from the thorns and thistles; but they were completely entangled amongst them. These, accordingly, thus entangled, pastured amongst the thorns and thistles, and were exceedingly miserable, being beaten by him; and he drove them hither and thither, and gave them no rest; and, altogether, these sheep were in a wretched plight.

Chapter 3

Seeing them, therefore, so beaten and so badly used, I was grieved
for them, because they were so tormented, and had no rest at all.
And I said to the Shepherd who talked with me, "Sir, who is this
shepherd, who is so pitiless and severe, and so completely devoid
of compassion for these sheep?" "This," he replied, "is the angel
of punishment; and he belongs to the just angels, and is appointed to punish. He accordingly takes those who wander away from
God, and who have walked in the desires and deceits of this
world, and chastises them as they deserve with terrible and
diverse punishments." "I would know, sir," I said, "Of what
nature are these diverse tortures and punishments?" "Hear," he
said, "the various tortures and punishments. The tortures are
such as occur during life. For some are punished with losses, others with want, others with sicknesses of various kinds, and others with all kinds of disorder and confusion; others are insulted
by unworthy persons, and exposed to suffering in many other
ways: for many, becoming unstable in their plans, try many
things, and none of them at all succeed, and they say they are not
prosperous in their undertakings; and it does not occur to their
minds that they have done evil deeds, but they blame the Lord.
When, therefore, they have been afflicted with all kinds of affliction, then are they delivered unto me for good training, and they
are made strong in the faith of the Lord; and for the rest of the
days of their life they are subject to the Lord with pure hearts,
and are successful in all their undertakings, obtaining from the

Lord everything they ask; and then they glorify the Lord, that they were delivered to me, and no longer suffer any evil."

Chapter 4

I said to him, "Sir, explain this also to me." "What is it you ask?" he said. "Whether, sir," I continued, "they who indulge in luxury, and who are deceived, are tortured for the same period of time that they have indulged in luxury and deceit?" He said to me, "They are tortured in the same manner." ["They are tormented much less, sir," I replied;] "for those who are so luxurious and who forget God ought to be tortured seven-fold." He said to me "You are foolish, and do not understand the power of torment." "Why, sir," I said, "if I had understood it, I would not have asked you to show me." "Hear," he said, "the power of both. The time of luxury and deceit is one hour; but the hour of torment is equivalent to thirty days. If, accordingly, a man indulge in luxury for one day, and be deceived and be tortured for one day, the day of his torture is equivalent to a whole year. For all the days of luxury, therefore, there are as many years of torture to be undergone. You see, then," he continued, "that the time of luxury and deceit is very short, but that of punishment and torture long.

Chapter 5

"Still," I said, "I do not quite understand about the time of deceit, and luxury, and torture; explain it to me more clearly." He answered, and said to me, "Your folly is persistent; and you do not wish to purify your heart, and serve God. Have a care," he added, "lest the time be fulfilled, and you be found foolish. Hear now," he added, "as you desire, that you may understand these things. He who indulges in luxury, and is deceived for one day, and who does what he wishes, is clothed with much foolishness, and does not understand the act which he does until the morrow; for he forgets what he did the day before. For luxury and deceit have no memories, on account of the folly with which they are clothed; but when punishment and torture cleave to a man for one day, he is punished and tortured for a year; for punishment and torture have powerful memories. While tortured and punished, therefore, for a whole year, he remembers at last his luxury and deceit, and knows that on their account he suffers evil. Every man, therefore, who is luxurious and deceived is thus tormented, because, although having life, they have given themselves over to death." "What kinds of luxury, sir," I asked, "are hurtful?" "Every act of a man which he performs with pleasure," he replied, "is an act of luxury; for the sharp-tempered man, when gratifying his tendency, indulges in luxury; and the adulterer, and the drunkard, and the back-biter, and the liar, and the covetous man, and the thief, and he who does things like these, gratifies his peculiar propensity, and in so doing indulges in luxury. All these acts of luxury are hurtful to the servants of God. On account of these deceits, therefore, do they suffer, who are punished and tortured. And there are also acts of luxury which save men; for many who do good indulge in luxury, being carried away by their own pleasure: this luxury, however, is beneficial to the servants of God, and gains life for such a man; but the injurious acts of luxury before enumerated bring tortures and punishment upon them; and if they continue in them and do not repent, they bring death upon themselves."

Seventh Similitude
They Who Repent
Must Bring Forth Fruits
Worthy of Repentance

∾

AFTER A FEW DAYS I saw him in the same plain where I had also seen the shepherds; and he said to me, "What do you wish with me?" I said to him, "Sir, that you would order the shepherd who punishes to depart out of my house, because he afflicts me exceedingly." "It is necessary," he replied, "that you be afflicted; for thus," he continued, "did the glorious angel command concerning you, as he wishes you to be tried." "What have I done which is so bad, sir," I replied, "that I should be delivered over to this angel?" "Listen," he said: "Your sins are many, but not so great as to require that you be delivered over to this angel; but your household has committed great iniquities and sins, and the glorious angel has been incensed at them on account of their deeds; and for this reason he commanded you to be afflicted for a certain time, that they also might repent, and purify themselves from every desire of this world. When, therefore, they repent and are purified, then the angel of punishment will depart." I said to him, "Sir, if they have done such things as to incense the glorious angel against them, yet what have I done?" He replied, "They cannot be afflicted at all, unless you, the head of the house, be afflicted: for when you are afflicted, of necessity they also suffer affliction; but if you are in comfort, they can feel no affliction." "Well, sir," I said, "they have repented with their whole heart." "I know, too," he answered, "that they have repented with their whole heart: do you think, however, that the sins of those who repent are remitted? Not altogether, but he who repents must torture his own soul, and be exceedingly humble in all his conduct, and be afflicted with many kinds of affliction; and if he endure the afflictions that come upon him, He who created all things, and endued them with power, will assuredly have compassion, and will heal him; and this will He do when He sees the heart of every penitent pure from every evil thing; and it is profitable for you and for your house to suffer affliction now. But why should I say much to you? You must be afflicted, as that angel of the Lord commanded who delivered you to me. And for this give thanks to the Lord, because He has deemed you worthy of showing you beforehand this affliction, that, knowing it before it comes, you may be able to bear it with courage." I said to him, "Sir, be thou with me, and I will be able to bear all affliction." "I will be with you," he said, "and I will ask the angel of punishment to afflict you more lightly; nevertheless, you will be afflicted for a little time, and again you will be re-established in your house. Only continue humble, and serve the Lord in all purity of heart, you and your children, and your house, and walk in my commands which I enjoin upon you, your repentance will be deep and pure; and if you observe these things with your household, every affliction will depart from you. And affliction," he added, "will depart from all who walk in these my commandments."

Eighth Similitude
The Sins of the Elect
and of the Penitent Are
of Many Kinds, But All Will
Be Rewarded According
to the Measure of Their
Repentance and Good Works

ᐒ

Chapter 1

HE SHOWED ME a large willow tree overshadowing plains and mountains, and under the shade of this willow had assembled all those who were called by the name of the Lord. And a glorious angel of the Lord, who was very tall, was standing beside the willow, having a large pruning-knife, and he was cutting little twigs from the willow and distributing them among the people that were overshadowed by the willow; and the twigs which he gave them were small, about a cubit, as it were, in length. And after they had all received the twigs, the angel laid down the pruning-knife, and that tree was sound, as I had seen it at first. And I marvelled within myself, saying, "How is the tree sound, after so many branches have been cut off?" And the Shepherd said to me, "Do not be surprised if the tree remains sound after so many branches were lopped off; [but wait,] and when you shall have seen everything, then it will be explained to you what it means."

The angel who had distributed the branches among the people again asked them from them, and in the order in which they had received them were they summoned to him, and each one of them returned his branch. And the angel of the Lord took and looked at them. From some he received the branches withered and moth-eaten; those who returned branches in that state the angel of the Lord ordered to stand apart. Others, again, returned them withered, but not moth-eaten; and these he ordered to stand apart. And others returned them half-withered, and these stood apart; and others returned their branches half-withered and having cracks in them, and these stood apart. [And others returned their branches green and having cracks in them; and these stood apart.] And others returned their branches, one-half withered and the other green; and these stood apart. And others brought their branches two-thirds green and the remaining third withered; and these stood apart. And others returned them two-thirds withered and one-third green; and these stood apart. And others returned their branches nearly all green, the smallest part only, the top, being withered, but they had cracks in them; and these stood apart. And of others very little was green, but the remaining parts withered; and these stood apart. And others came bringing their branches green, as they had received them from the angel. And the majority of the crowd returned branches of that kind, and with these the angel was exceedingly pleased; and these stood apart. [And others returned their branches green and having offshoots; and these stood apart, and with these the angel was exceedingly delighted.] And others returned their branches green and with offshoots, and the offshoots had some fruit, as it were; and those men whose branches were found to be of that kind were exceedingly joyful. And the angel was exultant because of them; and the Shepherd also rejoiced greatly because of them.

Chapter 2

And the angel of the Lord ordered crowns to be brought; and there were brought crowns, formed, as it were, of palms; and he crowned the men who had returned the branches which had off-shoots and some fruit, and sent them away into the tower. And the others also he sent into the tower, those, namely, who had returned branches that were green and had offshoots but no fruit, having given them seals. And all who went into the tower had the same clothing—white as snow. And those who returned their branches green, as they had received them, he set free, giving them clothing and seals. Now after the angel had finished these things, he said to the Shepherd, "I am going away, and you will send these away within the walls, according as each one is wor-thy to have his dwelling. And examine their branches carefully, and so dismiss them; but examine them with care. See that no one escape you," he added; "and if any escape you, I will try them at the altar." Having said these words to the Shepherd, he departed. And after the angel had departed, the Shepherd said to me, "Let us take the branches of all these and plant them, and see if any of them will live." I said to him, "Sir, how can these withered branches live?" He answered, and said, "This tree is a willow, and of a kind that is very tenacious of life. If, therefore, the branches be planted, and receive a little moisture, many of them will live. And now let us try, and pour water upon them; and if any of them live I shall rejoice with them, and if they do not I at least will not be found neglectful." And the Shepherd bade me call them as each one was placed. And they came, rank by rank, and gave their branches to the Shepherd. And the Shepherd received the branches, and planted them in rows; and after he had planted them he poured much water upon them, so that the branches could not be seen for the water; and after the branches had drunk it in, he said to me, "Let us go, and return after a few days, and inspect all the branches; for He who created this tree wishes all those to live who received branches from it. And I also hope that the greater part of these branches which received moisture and drank of the water will live."

Chapter 3

I said to him, "Sir, explain to me what this tree means, for I am perplexed about it, because, after so many branches have been cut off, it continues sound, and nothing appears to have been cut away from it. By this, now, I am perplexed." "Listen," he said: "This great tree that casts its shadow over plains, and mountains, and all the earth, is the law of God that was given to the whole world; and this law is the Son of God, proclaimed to the ends of the earth; and the people who are under its shadow are they who have heard the proclamation, and have believed upon Him. And the great and glorious angel Michael is he who has authority over this people, and governs them; for this is he who gave them the law into the hearts of believers: he accordingly superintends them to whom he gave it, to see if they have kept the same. And you see the branches of each one, for the branches are the law. You see, accordingly, many branches that have been rendered useless, and you will know them all—those who have not kept the law; and you will see the dwelling of each one." I said to him, "Sir, why did he dismiss some into the tower, and leave others to you?" "All," he answered, "who transgressed the law which they received from him, he left under my power for repentance; but all who have satisfied the law, and kept it, he retains under his own authority." "Who, then," I continued, "are they who were crowned, and who go to the tower?" "These are they who have suffered on account of the law; but the others, and they who returned their branches green, and with offshoots, but without fruit, are they who have been afflicted on account of the law, but who have not suffered nor denied their law; and they who returned their branches green as they had received them, are the venerable, and the just, and they who have walked carefully in a pure heart, and have kept the commandments of the Lord. And the rest you will know when I have examined those branches which have been planted and watered."

Chapter 4

And after a few days we came to the place, and the Shepherd sat down in the angel's place, and I stood beside him. And he said to me, "Gird yourself with pure, undressed linen made of sack-cloth;" and seeing me girded, and ready to minister to him, "Summon," he said, "the men to whom belong the branches that were planted, according to the order in which each one gave them in." So I went away to the plain, and summoned them all, and they all stood in their ranks. He said to them, "Let each one pull out his own branch, and bring it to me." The first to give in were those who had them withered and cut; and because they were found to be thus withered and cut, he commanded them to stand apart. And next they gave them in who had them withered, but not cut. And some of them gave in their branches green, and some withered and eaten as by a moth. Those that gave them in green, accordingly, he ordered to stand apart; and those who gave them in dry and cut, he ordered to stand along with the first. Next they gave them in who had them half-withered and cracked; and many of them gave them in green and without cracks; and some green and with offshoots and fruits upon the offshoots, such as they had who went, after being crowned, into the tower. And some handed them in withered and eaten, and some withered and uneaten; and some as they were, half-withered and cracked. And he commanded them each one to stand apart, some towards their own rows, and others apart from them.

Chapter 5

Then they gave in their branches who had them green, but cracked: all these gave them in green, and stood in their own row. And the Shepherd was pleased with these, because they were all changed, and had lost their cracks. And they also gave them in who had them half-green and half-withered: of some, accordingly, the branches were found completely green; of others, half-withered; of others, withered and eaten; of others, green, and having offshoots. All these were sent away, each to his own row. [Next they gave in who had them two parts green and one-third withered. Many of them gave them half-withered; and others withered and rotten; and others half-withered and cracked, and a few green. These all stood in their own row.] And they gave them in who had them green, but to a very slight extent withered and cracked. Of these, some gave them in green, and others green and with offshoots. And these also went away to their own row. Next they gave them who had a very small part green and the other parts withered. Of these the branches were found for the most part green and having offshoots, and fruit upon the offshoots, and others altogether green. With these branches the Shepherd was exceedingly pleased, because they were found in this state. And these went away, each to his own row.

Chapter 6

After the Shepherd had examined the branches of them all, he said to me, "I told you that this tree was tenacious of life. You see," he continued, "how many repented and were saved." "I see, sir," I replied. "That you may behold," he added, "the great mercy of the Lord, that it is great and glorious, and that He has given His Spirit to those who are worthy of repentance." "Why then, sir," I said, "did not all these repent?" He answered, "To them whose heart He saw would become pure, and obedient to Him, He gave power to repent with the whole heart. But to them whose deceit and wickedness He perceived, and saw that they intended to repent hypocritically, He did not grant repentance, lest they should again profane His name." I said to him, "Sir, show me now, with respect to those who gave in the branches, of what sort they are, and their abode, in order that they hearing it who believed, and received the seal, and broke it, and did not keep it whole, may, on coming to a knowledge of their deeds, repent, and receive from you a seal, and may glorify the Lord because He had compassion upon them, and sent you to renew their spirits." "Listen," he said: "they whose branches were found withered and moth-eaten are the apostates and traitors of the Church, who have blasphemed the Lord in their sins, and have, moreover, been ashamed of the name of the Lord by which they were called. These, therefore, at the end were lost unto God. And you see that not a single one of them repented, although they heard the words which I spake to them, which I enjoined upon you. From such life departed. And they who gave them in withered and undecayed, these also were near to them; for they were hypocrites, and introducers of strange doctrines, and subverters of the servants of God, especially of those who had sinned, not allowing them to repent, but persuading them by foolish doctrines. These, accordingly, have a hope of repentance. And you see that many of them also have repented since I spake to them, and they will still repent. But all who will not repent have lost their lives; and as many of them as repented became good, and their dwelling was appointed within the first walls; and some of them ascended even into the tower. You see, then," he said, "that repentance involves life to sinners, but non-repentance death."

Chapter 7

"And as many as gave in the branches half-withered and cracked, hear also about them. They whose branches were half-withered to the same extent are the wavering; for they neither live, nor are they dead. And they who have them half-withered and cracked are both waverers and slanderers, [railing against the absent,] and never at peace with one another, but always at variance. And yet to these also," he continued, "repentance is possible. You see," he said, "that some of them have repented, and there is still remaining in them," he continued, "a hope of repentance. And as many of them," he added, "as have repented, shall have their dwelling in the tower. And those of them who have been slower in repenting shall dwell within the walls. And as many as do not repent at all, but abide in their deeds, shall utterly perish. And they who gave in their branches green and cracked were always faithful and good, though emulous of each other about the foremost places, and about fame: now all these are foolish, in indulging in such a rivalry. Yet they also, being naturally good, on hearing my commandments, purified themselves, and soon repented. Their dwelling, accordingly, was in the tower. But if any one relapse into strife, he will be cast out of the tower, and will lose his life. Life is the possession of all who keep the commandments of the Lord; but in the commandments there is no rivalry in regard to the first places, or glory of any kind, but in regard to patience and personal humility. Among such persons, then, is the life of the Lord, but amongst the quarrelsome and transgressors, death."

Chapter 8

"And they who gave in their branches half-green and half-withered, are those who are immersed in business, and do not cleave to the saints. For this reason, the one half of them is living, and the other half dead. Many, accordingly, who heard my commands repented, and those at least who repented had their dwelling in the tower. But some of them at last fell away: these, accordingly, have not repentance, for on account of their business they blasphemed the Lord, and denied Him. They therefore lost their lives through the wickedness which they committed. And many of them doubted. These still have repentance in their power, if they repent speedily; and their abode will be in the tower. But if they are slower in repenting, they will dwell within the walls; and if they do not repent, they too have lost their lives. And they who gave in their branches two-thirds withered and one-third green, are those who have denied [the Lord] in various ways. Many, however, repented, but some of them hesitated and were in doubt. These, then, have repentance within their reach, if they repent quickly, and do not remain in their pleasures; but if they abide in their deeds, these, too, work to themselves death."

Chapter 9

"And they who returned their branches two-thirds withered and one-third green, are those that were faithful indeed; but after acquiring wealth, and becoming distinguished amongst the heathen, they clothed themselves with great pride, and became lofty-minded, and deserted the truth, and did not cleave to the righteous, but lived with the heathen, and this way of life became more agreeable to them. They did not, however, depart from God, but remained in the faith, although not working the works of faith. Many of them accordingly repented, and their dwelling was in the tower. And others continuing to live until the end with the heathen, and being corrupted by their vain glories, [departed from God, serving the works and deeds of the heathen.] These were reckoned with the heathen. But others of them hesitated, not hoping to be saved on account of the deeds which they had done; while others were in doubt, and caused divisions among themselves. To those, therefore, who were in doubt on account of their deeds, repentance is still open; but their repentance ought to be speedy, that their dwelling may be in the tower. And to those who do not repent, but abide in their pleasures, death is near."

Chapter 10

"And they who give in their branches green, but having the tips withered and cracked, these were always good, and faithful, and distinguished before God; but they sinned a very little through indulging small desires, and finding little faults with one another. But on hearing my words the greater part of them quickly repented, and their dwelling was upon the tower. Yet some of them were in doubt; and certain of them who were in doubt wrought greater dissension. Among these, therefore, is hope of repentance, because they were always good; and with difficulty will any one of them perish. And they who gave up their branches withered, but having a very small part green, are those who believed only, yet continue working the works of iniquity. They never, however, departed from God, but gladly bore His name, and joyfully received His servants into their houses. Having accordingly heard of this repentance, they unhesitatingly repented, and practice all virtue and righteousness; and some of them even [suffered, being willingly put to death], knowing their deeds which they had done. Of all these, therefore, the dwelling shall be in the tower."

Chapter 11

And after he had finished the explanations of all the branches, he said to me, "Go and tell them to everyone, that they may repent, and they shall live unto God. Because the Lord, having had compassion on all men, has sent me to give repentance, although some are not worthy of it on account of their works; but the Lord, being long-suffering, desires those who were called by His Son to be saved." I said to him, "Sir, I hope that all who have heard them will repent; for I am persuaded that each one, on coming to a knowledge of his own works, and fearing the Lord, will repent." He answered me, and said, "All who with their whole heart shall purify themselves from their wickedness before enumerated, and shall add no more to their sins, will receive healing from the Lord for their former transgressions, if they do not hesitate at these commandments; and they will live unto God. But do you walk in my commandments, and live." Having shown me these things, and spoken all these words, he said to me, "And the rest I will show you after a few days."

Ninth Similitude
The Great Mysteries in
the Building of the Militant
and Triumphant Church

∾

Chapter 1

AFTER I HAD WRITTEN down the commandments and similitudes of the Shepherd, the angel of repentance, he came to me and said, "I wish to explain to you what the Holy Spirit that spake with you in the form of the Church showed you, for that Spirit is the Son of God. For, as you were somewhat weak in the flesh, it was not explained to you by the angel. When, however, you were strengthened by the Spirit, and your strength was increased, so that you were able to see the angel also, then accordingly was the building of the tower shown you by the Church. In a noble and solemn manner did you see everything as if shown you by a virgin; but now you see [them] through the same Spirit as if shown by an angel. You must, however, learn everything from me with greater accuracy. For I was sent for this purpose by the glorious angel to dwell in your house, that you might see all things with power, entertaining no fear, even as it was before." And he led me away into Arcadia, to a round hill; and he placed me on the top of the hill, and showed me a large plain, and round about the plain twelve mountains, all having different forms. The first was black as soot; and the second bare, without grass; and the third full of thorns and thistles; and the fourth with grass half-withered, the upper parts of the plants green, and the parts about the roots withered; and some of the grasses, when the sun scorched them, became withered. And the fifth mountain had green grass, and was ragged. And the sixth mountain was quite full of clefts, some small and others large; and the clefts were grassy, but the plants were not very vigorous, but rather, as it were, decayed. The seventh mountain, again, had cheerful pastures, and the whole mountain was blooming, and every kind of cattle and birds were feeding upon that mountain; and the more the cattle and the birds ate, the more the grass of that mountain flourished. And the eighth mountain was full of fountains, and every kind of the Lord's creatures drank of the fountains of that mountain. But the ninth mountain [had no water at all, and was wholly a desert, and had within it deadly serpents, which destroy men. And the tenth mountain] had very large trees, and was completely shaded, and under the shadow of the trees sheep lay resting and ruminating. And the eleventh mountain was very thickly wooded, and those trees were productive, being adorned with various sorts of fruits, so that any one seeing them would desire to eat of their fruits. The twelfth mountain, again, was wholly white, and its aspect was cheerful, and the mountain in itself was very beautiful.

Chapter 2

And in the middle of the plain he showed me a large white rock that had arisen out of the plain. And the rock was more lofty than the mountains, rectangular in shape, so as to be capable of containing the whole world: and that rock was old, having a gate cut out of it; and the cutting out of the gate seemed to me as if recently done. And the gate glittered to such a degree under the sunbeams, that I marvelled at the splendor of the gate; and round about the gate were standing twelve virgins. The four who stood at the corners seemed to me more distinguished than the others—they were all, however, distinguished—and they were standing at the four parts of the gate; two virgins between each part. And they were clothed with linen tunics, and gracefully girded, having their right shoulders exposed, as if about to bear some burden. Thus they stood ready; for they were exceedingly cheerful and eager. After I had seen these things, I marvelled in myself, because I was beholding great and glorious sights. And again I was perplexed about the virgins, because, although so delicate, they were standing courageously, as if about to carry the whole heavens. And the Shepherd said to me "Why are you reasoning in yourself, and perplexing your mind, and distressing yourself? for the things which you cannot understand, do not attempt to comprehend, as if you were wise; but ask the Lord, that you may receive understanding and know them. You cannot see what is behind you, but you see what is before. Whatever, then, you cannot see, let alone, and do not torment yourself about it: but what you see, make yourself master of it, and do not waste your labour about other things; and I will explain to you everything that I show you. Look therefore, on the things that remain."

Chapter 3

I saw six men come, tall, and distinguished, and similar in appearance, and they summoned a multitude of men. And they who came were also tall men, and handsome, and powerful; and the six men commanded them to build a tower above the rock. And great was the noise of those men who came to build the tower, as they ran hither and thither around the gate. And the virgins who stood around the gate told the men to hasten to build the tower. Now the virgins had spread out their hands, as if about to receive something from the men. And the six men commanded stones to ascend out of a certain pit, and to go to the building of the tower. And there went up ten shining rectangular stones, not hewn in a quarry. And the six men called the virgins, and bade them carry all the stones that were intended for the building, and to pass through the gate, and give them to the men who were about to build the tower. And the virgins put upon one another the ten first stones which had ascended from the pit, and carried them together, each stone by itself.

Chapter 4

And as they stood together around the gate, those who seemed to be strong carried them, and they stooped down under the corners of the stone; and the others stooped down under the sides of the stones. And in this way they carried all the stones. And they carried them through the gate as they were commanded, and gave them to the men for the tower; and they took the stones and proceeded with the building. Now the tower was built upon the great rock, and above the gate. Those ten stones were prepared as the foundation for the building of the tower. And the rock and gate were the support of the whole of the tower. And after the ten stones other twenty [five] came up out of the pit, and these were fitted into the building of the tower, being earned by the virgins as before. And after these ascended thirty-five. And these in like manner were fitted into the tower. And after these other forty stones came up; and all these were cast into the building of the tower, [and there were four rows in the foundation of the tower,] and they ceased ascending from the pit. And the builders also ceased for a little. And again the six men commanded the multitude of the crowd to bear stones from the mountains for the building of the tower.

They were accordingly brought from all the mountains of various colours, and being hewn by the men were given to the virgins; and the virgins carried them through the gate, and gave them for the building of the tower. And when the stones of various colours were placed in the building, they all became white alike, and lost their different colours. And certain stones were given by the men for the building, and these did not become shining; but as they were placed, such also were they found to remain: for they were not given by the virgins, nor carried through the gate. These stones, therefore, were not in keeping with the others in the building of the tower. And the six men, seeing these unsuitable stones in the building, commanded them to be taken away, and to be carried away down to their own place whence they had been taken; [and being removed one by one, they were laid aside; and] they say to the men who brought the stones, "Do not ye bring any stones at all for the building, but lay them down beside the tower, that the virgins may carry them through the gate, and may give them for the building. For unless," they said, "they be carried through the gate by the hands of the virgins, they cannot change their colours: do not toil, therefore," they said, "to no purpose."

Chapter 5

And on that day the building was finished, but the tower was not completed; for additional building was again about to be added, and there was a cessation in the building. And the six men commanded the builders all to withdraw a little distance, and to rest, but enjoined the virgins not to withdraw from the tower; and it seemed to me that the virgins had been left to guard the tower. Now after all had withdrawn, and were resting themselves, I said to the Shepherd, "What is the reason that the building of the tower was not finished?" "The tower," he answered, "cannot be finished just yet, until the Lord of it come and examine the building, in order that, if any of the stones be found to be decayed, he may change them: for the tower is built according to his pleasure." "I would like to know, sir," I said, "what is the meaning of the building of this tower, and what the rock and gate, and the mountains, and the virgins mean, and the stones that ascended from the pit, and were not hewn, but came as they were to the building. Why, in the first place, were ten stones placed in the foundation, then twenty-five, then thirty-five, then forty? and I wish also to know about the stones that went to the building, and were again taken out and returned to their own place? On all these points put my mind at rest, sir, and explain them to me." "If you are not found to be curious about trifles," he replied, "you shall know everything. For after a few days [we shall come hither, and you will see the other things that happen to this tower, and will know accurately all the similitudes." After a few days] we came to the place where we sat down. And he said to me, "Let us go to the tower; for the master of the tower is coming to examine it." And we came to the tower, and there was no one at all near it, save the virgins only. And the Shepherd asked the virgins if perchance the master of the tower had come; and they replied that he was about to come to examine the building.

Chapter 6

And, behold, after a little I see an array of many men coming, and in the midst of them one man of so remarkable a size as to overtop the tower. And the six men who had worked upon the building were with him, and many other honourable men were around him. And the virgins who kept the tower ran forward and kissed him, and began to walk near him around the tower. And that man examined the building carefully, feeling every stone separately; and holding a rod in his hand, he struck every stone in the building three times. And when he struck them, some of them became black as soot, and some appeared as if covered with scabs, and some cracked, and some mutilated, and some neither white nor black, and some rough and not in keeping with the other stones, and some having [very many] stains: such were the varieties of decayed stones that were found in the building. He ordered all these to be taken out of the tower, and to be laid down beside it, and other stones to be brought and put in their stead. [And the builders asked him from what mountain he wished them to be brought and put in their place.] And he did not command them to be brought from the mountains, [but he bade them be brought from a certain plain which was near at hand.] And the plain was dug up, and shining rectangular stones were found, and some also of a round shape; and all the stones which were in that plain were brought, and carried through the gate by the virgins. And the rectangular stones were hewn, and put in place of those that were taken away; but the rounded stones were not put into the building, because they were hard to hew, and appeared to yield slowly to the chisel; they were deposited, however, beside the tower, as if intended to be hewn and used in the building, for they were exceedingly brilliant.

Chapter 7

The glorious man, the lord of the whole tower, having according-ly finished these alterations, called to him the Shepherd, and delivered to him all the stones that were lying beside the tower, that had been rejected from the building, and said to him, "Carefully clean all these stones, and put aside such for the build-ing of the tower as may harmonize with the others; and those that do not, throw far away from the tower." [Having given these orders to the Shepherd, he departed from the tower], with all those with whom he had come. Now the virgins were standing around the tower, keeping it. I said again to the Shepherd, "Can these stones return to the building of the tower, after being reject-ed?" He answered me, and said, "Do you see these stones?" "I see them, sir," I replied. "The greater part of these stones," he said, "I will hew, and put into the building, and they will harmonize with the others." "How, sir," I said, "can they, after being cut all round about, fill up the same space?" He answered, "Those that shall be found small will be thrown into the middle of the build-ing, and those that are larger will be placed on the outside, and they will hold them together." Having spoken these words, he said to me, "Let us go, and after two days let us come and clean these stones, and cast them into the building; for all things around the tower must be cleaned, lest the Master come sudden-ly and find the places about the tower dirty, and be displeased, and these stones be not returned for the building of the tower, and I also shall seem to be neglectful towards the Master." And after two days we came to the tower, and he said to me, "Let us examine all the stones, and ascertain those which may return to the building." I said to him, "Sir, let us examine them!"

Chapter 8

And beginning, we first examined the black stones. And such as they had been taken out of the building were they found to remain; and the Shepherd ordered them to be removed out of the tower, and to be placed apart. Next he examined those that had scabs; and he took and hewed many of these, and commanded the virgins to take them up and cast them into the building. And the virgins lifted them up, and put them in the middle of the building of the tower. And the rest he ordered to be laid down beside the black ones; for these, too, were found to be black. He next examined those that had cracks; and he hewed many of these, and commanded them to be carried by the virgins to the building: and they were placed on the outside, because they were found to be sounder than the others; but the rest, on account of the multitude of the cracks, could not be hewn, and for this reason, therefore, they were rejected from the building of the tower. He next examined the chipped stones, and many amongst these were found to be black, and some to have great cracks. And these also he commanded to be laid down along with those which had been rejected. But the remainder, after being cleaned and hewn, he commanded to be placed in the building. And the virgins took them up, and fitted them into the middle of the building of the tower, for they were somewhat weak. He next examined those that were half white and half black, and many of them were found to be black. And he commanded these also to be taken away along with those which had been rejected. And the rest were all taken away by the virgins; for, being white, they were fitted by the virgins themselves into the building. And they were placed upon the outside, because they were found to be sound, so as to be able to support those which were placed in the middle, for no part of them at all was chipped. He next examined those that were rough and hard; and a few of them were rejected because they could not be hewn, as they were found exceedingly hard. But the rest of them were hewn, and carried by the virgins, and fitted into the middle of the building of the tower; for they were somewhat weak. He next examined those that had stains; and of these a very few were black, and were thrown aside with the others; but the greater part were found to be bright, and these were fitted by the virgins into the building, but on account of their strength were placed on the outside.

Chapter 9

He next came to examine the white and rounded stones, and said to me, "What are we to do with these stones?" "How do I know, sir?" I replied. "Have you no intentions regarding them?" "Sir," I answered, "I am not acquainted with this art, neither am I a stone-cutter, nor can I tell." "Do you not see," he said, "that they are exceedingly round? and if I wish to make them rectangular, a large portion of them must be cut away; for some of them must of necessity be put into the building." "If therefore," I said, "they must, why do you torment yourself, and not at once choose for the building those which you prefer, and fit them into it?" He selected the larger ones among them, and the shining ones, and hewed them; and the virgins carried and fitted them into the outside parts of the building. And the rest which remained over were carried away, and laid down on the plain from which they were brought. They were not, however, rejected, "because," he said, "there remains yet a little addition to be built to the tower. And the lord of this tower wishes all the stones to be fitted into the building, because they are exceedingly bright." And twelve women were called, very beautiful in form, clothed in black, and with dishevelled hair. And these women seemed to me to be fierce. But the Shepherd commanded them to lift the stones that were rejected from the building, and to carry them away to the mountains from which they had been brought. And they were merry, and carried away all the stones, and put them in the place whence they had been taken. Now after all the stones were removed, and there was no longer a single one lying around the tower, he said, "Let us go round the tower and see, lest there be any defect in it." So I went round the tower along with him. And the Shepherd, seeing that the tower was beautifully built, rejoiced exceedingly; for the tower was built in such a way, that, on seeing it, I coveted the building of it, for it was constructed as if built of one stone, without a single joining. And the stone seemed as if hewn out of the rock; having to me the appearance of a monolith.

Chapter 10

And as I walked along with him, I was full of joy, beholding so many excellent things. And the Shepherd said to me, "Go and bring unslacked lime and fine-baked clay, that I may fill up the forms of the stones that were taken and thrown into the building; for everything about the tower must be smooth." And I did as he commanded me, and brought it to him. "Assist me," he said, "and the work will soon be finished." He accordingly filled up the forms of the stones that were returned to the building, and commanded the places around the tower to be swept and to be cleaned; and the virgins took brooms and swept the place, and carried all the dirt out of the tower, and brought water, and the ground around the tower became cheerful and very beautiful. Says the Shepherd to me, "Everything has been cleared away; if the lord of the tower come to inspect it, he can have no fault to find with us." Having spoken these words, he wished to depart; but I laid hold of him by the wallet, and began to adjure him by the Lord that he would explain what he had showed me. He said to me, "I must rest a little, and then I shall explain to you everything; wait for me here until I return." I said to him, "Sir, what can I do here alone?" "You are not alone," he said, "for these virgins are with you." "Give me in charge to them, then," I replied. The Shepherd called them to him, and said to them, "I entrust him to you until I come," and went away. And I was alone with the virgins; and they were rather merry, but were friendly to me, especially the four more distinguished of them.

Chapter 11

The virgins said to me, "The Shepherd does not come here today." "What, then," said I, "am I to do?" They replied, "Wait for him until he comes; and if he comes he will converse with you, and if he does not come you will remain here with us until he does come." I said to them, "I will wait for him until it is late; and if he does not arrive, I will go away into the house, and come back early in the morning." And they answered and said to me, "You were entrusted to us; you cannot go away from us." "Where, then," I said, "am I to remain?" "You will sleep with us," they replied, "as a brother, and not as a husband: for you are our brother, and for the time to come we intend to abide with you, for we love you exceedingly!" But I was ashamed to remain with them. And she who seemed to be the first among them began to kiss me. [And the others seeing her kissing me, began also to kiss me], and to lead me round the tower, and to play with me. And I, too, became like a young man, and began to play with them: for some of them formed a chorus, and others danced, and others sang; and I, keeping silence, walked with them around the tower, and was merry with them. And when it grew late I wished to go into the house; and they would not let me, but detained me. So I remained with them during the night, and slept beside the tower. Now the virgins spread their linen tunics on the ground, and made me lie down in the midst of them; and they did nothing at all but pray; and I without ceasing prayed with them, and not less than they. And the virgins rejoiced because I thus prayed. And I remained there with the virgins until the next day at the second hour. Then the Shepherd returned, and said to the virgins, "Did you offer him any insult?" "Ask him," they said. I said to him, "Sir, I was delighted that I remained with them." "On what," he asked, "did you sup?" "I supped, sir," I replied, "on the words of the Lord the whole night." "Did they receive you well?" he inquired. "Yes, sir," I answered. "Now," he said, "what do you wish to hear first?" "I wish to hear in the order," I said, "in which you showed me from the beginning. I beg of you, sir, that as I shall ask you, so also you will give me the explanation." "As you wish," he replied, "so also will I explain to you, and will conceal nothing at all from you."

Chapter 12

"First of all, sir," I said, "explain this to me: What is the meaning of the rock and the gate?" "This rock," he answered, "and this gate are the Son of God." "How, sir?" I said; "the rock is old, and the gate is new." "Listen," he said, "and understand, O ignorant man. The Son of God is older than all His creatures, so that He was a fellow-councillor with the Father in His work of creation; for this reason is He old." "And why is the gate new, sir?" I said. "Because," he answered, "He became manifest in the last days of the dispensation: for this reason the gate was made new, that they who are to be saved by it might enter into the kingdom of God. You saw," he said, "that those stones which came in through the gate were used for the building of the tower, and that those which did not come, were again thrown back to their own place?" "I saw, sir," I replied. "In like manner," he continued, "no one shall enter into the kingdom of God unless he receive His holy name. For if you desire to enter into a city, and that city is surrounded by a wall, and has but one gate, can you enter into that city save through the gate which it has?" "Why, how can it be otherwise, sir?" I said. "If, then, you cannot enter into the city except through its gate, so, in like manner, a man cannot otherwise enter into the kingdom of God than by the name of His beloved Son. You saw," he added, "the multitude who were building the tower?" "I saw them, sir," I said. "Those," he said, "are all glorious angels, and by them accordingly is the Lord surrounded. And the gate is the Son of God. This is the one entrance to the Lord. In no other way, then, shall any one enter in to Him except through His Son. You saw," he continued, "the six men, and the tall and glorious man in the midst of them, who walked round the tower, and rejected the stones from the building?" "I saw him, sir," I answered. "The glorious man," he said, "is the Son of God, and those six glorious angels are those who support Him on the right hand and on the left. None of these glorious angels," he continued, "will enter in unto God apart from Him. Whosoever does not receive His name, shall not enter into the kingdom of God."

Chapter 13

"And the tower," I asked, "what does it mean?" "This tower," he replied, "is the Church." "And these virgins, who are they?" "They are holy spirits, and men cannot otherwise be found in the kingdom of God unless these have put their clothing upon them: for if you receive the name only, and do not receive from them the clothing, they are of no advantage to you. For these virgins are the powers of the Son of God. If you bear His name but possess not His power, it will be in vain that you bear His name. Those stones," he continued, "which you saw rejected bore His name, but did not put on the clothing of the virgins." "Of what nature is their clothing, sir?" I asked. "Their very names," he said, "are their clothing. Every one who bears the name of the Son of God, ought to bear the names also of these; for the Son Himself bears the names of these virgins. As many stones," he continued, "as you saw [come into the building of the tower through the hands] of these virgins, and remaining, have been clothed with their strength. For this reason you see that the tower became of one stone with the rock. So also they who have believed on the Lord through His Son, and are clothed with these spirits, shall become one spirit, one body, and the colour of their garments shall be one. And the dwelling of such as bear the names of the virgins is in the tower." "Those stones, sir, that were rejected," I inquired, "on what account were they rejected? for they passed through the gate, and were placed by the hands of the virgins in the building of the tower." "Since you take an interest in everything," he replied, "and examine minutely, hear about the stones that were rejected. These all," he said, "received the name of God, and they received also the strength of these virgins. Having received, then, these spirits, they were made strong, and were with the servants of God; and theirs was one spirit, and one body, and one clothing. For they were of the same mind, and wrought righteousness. After a certain time, however, they were persuaded by the women whom you saw clothed in black, and having their shoulders exposed and their hair dishevelled, and beautiful in appearance. Having seen these women, they desired to have them, and clothed themselves with their strength, and put off the strength of the virgins. These, accordingly, were rejected from the house of God, and were given over to these women. But they who were not deceived by the beauty of these women remained in the house of God. You have," he said, "the explanation of those who were rejected."

Chapter 14

"What, then, sir," I said, "if these men, being such as they are, repent and put away their desires after these women, and return again to the virgins, and walk in their strength and in their works, shall they not enter into the house of God?" "They shall enter in," he said, "if they put away the works of these women, and put on again the strength of the virgins, and walk in their works. For on this account was there a cessation in the building, in order that, if these repent, they may depart into the building of the tower. But if they do not repent, then others will come in their place, and these at the end will be cast out. For all these things I gave thanks to the Lord, because He had pity on all that call upon His name; and sent the angel of repentance to us who sinned against Him, and renewed our spirit; and when we were already destroyed, and had no hope of life, He restored us to newness of life." "Now, sir," I continued, "show me why the tower was not built upon the ground, but upon the rock and upon the gate." "Are you still," he said, "without sense and understanding?" "I must, sir," I said, "ask you of all things, because I am wholly unable to understand them; for all these things are great and glorious, and difficult for man to understand." "Listen," he said: "the name of the Son of God is great, and cannot be contained, and supports the whole world. If, then, the whole creation is supported by the Son of God, what think ye of those who are called by Him, and bear the name of the Son of God, and walk in His commandments? Do you see what kind of persons He supports? Those who bear His name with their whole heart. He Himself, accordingly, became a foundation to them, and supports them with joy, because they are not ashamed to bear His name."

Chapter 15

"Explain to me, sir," I said, "the names of these virgins, and of those women who were clothed in black raiment." "Hear," he said, "the names of the stronger virgins who stood at the corners. The first is Faith, the second Continence, the third Power, the fourth Patience. And the others standing in the midst of these have the following names: Simplicity, Innocence, Purity, Cheerfulness, Truth, Understanding, Harmony, Love. He who bears these names and that of the Son of God will be able to enter into the kingdom of God. Hear, also," he continued, "the names of the women who had the black garments; and of these four are stronger than the rest. The first is Unbelief, the second: Incontinence, the third Disobedience, the fourth Deceit. And their followers are called Sorrow, Wickedness, Wantonness, Anger, Falsehood, Folly, Backbiting, Hatred. The servant of God who bears these names shall see, indeed, the kingdom of God, but shall not enter into it." "And the stones, sir," I said, "which were taken out of the pit and fitted into the building: what are they?" "The first," he said, "the ten, viz., that were placed as a foundation, are the first generation, and the twenty-five the second generation, of righteous men; and the thirty-five are the prophets of God and His ministers; and the forty are the apostles and teachers of the preaching of the Son of God." "Why, then, sir," I asked, "did the virgins carry these stones also through the gate, and give them for the building of the tower?" "Because," he answered, "these were the first who bore these spirits, and they never departed from each other, neither the spirits from the men nor the men from the spirits, but the spirits remained with them until their falling asleep. And unless they had had these spirits with them, they would not have been of use for the building of this tower."

Chapter 16

"Explain to me a little further, sir," I said. "What is it that you desire?" he asked. "Why, sir," I said, "did these stones ascend out of the pit, and be applied to the building of the tower, after having borne these spirits?" "They were obliged," he answered, "to ascend through water in order that they might be made alive; for, unless they laid aside the deadness of their life, they could not in any other way enter into the kingdom of God. Accordingly, those also who fell asleep received the seal of the Son of God. For," he continued, "before a man bears the name of the Son of God he is dead; but when he receives the seal he lays aside his deadness, and obtains life. The seal, then, is the water: they descend into the water dead, and they arise alive. And to them, accordingly, was this seal preached, and they made use of it that they might enter into the kingdom of God." "Why, sir," I asked, "did the forty stones also ascend with them out of the pit, having already received the seal?" "Because," he said, "these apostles and teachers who preached the name of the Son of God, after falling asleep in the power and faith of the Son of God, preached it not only to those who were asleep, but themselves also gave them the seal of the preaching. Accordingly they descended with them into the water, and again ascended. [But these descended alive and rose up again alive; whereas they who had previously fallen asleep descended dead, but rose up again alive.] By these, then, were they quickened and made to know the name of the Son of God. For this reason also did they ascend with them, and were fitted along with them into the building of the tower, and, untouched by the chisel, were built in along with them. For they slept in righteousness and in great purity, but only they had not this seal. You have accordingly the explanation of these also."

Chapter 17

"I understand, sir," I replied. "Now, sir," I continued, "explain to me, with respect to the mountains, why their forms are various and diverse." "Listen," he said: "these mountains are the twelve tribes, which inhabit the whole world. The Son of God, accordingly, was preached unto them by the apostles." "But why are the mountains of various kinds, some having one form, and others another? Explain that to me, sir." "Listen," he answered: "these twelve tribes that inhabit the whole world are twelve nations. And they vary in prudence and understanding. As numerous, then, as are the varieties of the mountains which you saw, are also the diversities of mind and understanding among these nations. And I will explain to you the actions of each one." "First, sir," I said, "explain this: why, when the mountains are so diverse, their stones, when placed in the building, became one colour, shining like those also that had ascended out of the pit." "Because," he said, "all the nations that dwell under heaven were called by hearing and believing upon the name of the Son of God. Having, therefore, received the seal, they had one understanding and one mind; and their faith became one, and their love one, and with the name they bore also the spirits of the virgins. On this account the building of the tower became of one colour, bright as the sun. But after they had entered into the same place, and became one body, certain of these defiled themselves, and were expelled from the race of the righteous, and became again what they were before, or rather worse."

Chapter 18

"How, sir," I said, "did they become worse, after having known God?" "He that does not know God," he answered, "and practices evil, receives a certain chastisement for his wickedness; but he that has known God, ought not any longer to do evil, but to do good. If, accordingly, when he ought to do good, he do evil, does not he appear to do greater evil than he who does not know God? For this reason, they who have not known God and do evil are condemned to death; but they who have known God, and have seen His mighty works, and still continue in evil, shall be chastised doubly, and shall die for ever. In this way, then, will the Church of God be purified. For as you saw the stones rejected from the tower, and delivered to the evil spirits, and cast out thence, so [they also shall be cast out, and] there shall be one body of the purified; as the tower also became, as it were, of one stone after its purification. In like manner also shall it be with the Church of God, after it has been purified, and has rejected the wicked, and the hypocrites, and the blasphemers, and the waverers, and those who commit wickedness of different kinds. After these have been cast away, the Church of God shall be one body, of one mind, of one understanding, of one faith, of one love. And then the Son of God will be exceeding glad, and shall rejoice over them, because He has received His people pure." "All these things, sir," I said, "are great and glorious."

"Moreover, sir," I said, "explain to me the power and the actions of each one of the mountains, that every soul, trusting in the Lord, and hearing it, may glorify His great, and marvellous, and glorious name." "Hear," he said, "the diversity of the mountains and of the twelve nations."

Chapter 19

"From the first mountain, which was black, they that believed are the following: apostates and blasphemers against the Lord, and betrayers of the servants of God. To these repentance is not open; but death lies before them, and on this account also are they black, for their race is a lawless one. And from the second mountain, which was bare, they who believed are the following: hypocrites, and teachers of wickedness. And these, accordingly, are like the former, not having any fruits of righteousness; for as their mountain was destitute of fruit, so also such men have a name indeed, but are empty of faith, and there is no fruit of truth in them. They indeed have repentance in their power, if they repent quickly; but if they are slow in so doing, they shall die along with the former." "Why, sir," I said, "have these repentance, but the former not? for their actions are nearly the same." "On this account," he said, "have these repentance, because they did not blaspheme their Lord, nor become betrayers of the servants of God; but on account of their desire of possessions they became hypocritical, and each one taught according to the desires of men that were sinners. But they will suffer a certain punishment; and repentance is before them, because they were not blasphemers or traitors."

Chapter 20

"And from the third mountain, which had thorns and thistles, they who believed are the following. There are some of them rich, and others immersed in much business. The thistles are the rich, and the thorns are they who are immersed in much business. Those, [accordingly, who are entangled in many various kinds of business, do not] cleave to the servants of God, but wander away, being choked by their business transactions; and the rich cleave with difficulty to the servants of God, fearing lest these should ask something of them. Such persons, accordingly, shall have difficulty in entering the kingdom of God. For as it is disagreeable to walk among thistles with naked feet, so also it is hard for such to enter the kingdom of God. But to all these repentance, and that speedy, is open, in order that what they did not do in former times they may make up for in these days, and do some good, and they shall live unto God. But if they abide in their deeds, they shall be delivered to those women, who will put them to death."

Chapter 21

"And from the fourth mountain, which had much grass, the upper parts of the plants green, and the parts about the roots withered, and some also scorched by the sun, they who believed are the following: the doubtful, and they who have the Lord upon their lips, but have Him not in their heart. On this account their foundations are withered, and have no strength; and their words alone live, while their works are dead. Such persons are [neither alive nor] dead. They resemble, therefore, the waverers: for the wavering are neither withered nor green, being neither living nor dead. For as their blades, on seeing the sun, were withered, so also the wavering, when they hear of affliction, on account of their fear, worship idols, and are ashamed of the name of their Lord. Such, then, are neither alive nor dead. But these also may yet live, if they repent quickly; and if they do not repent, they are already delivered to women, who take away their life."

Chapter 22

"And from the fifth mountain, which had green grass, and was rugged, they who believed are the following: believers, indeed, but slow to learn, and obstinate, and pleasing themselves, wishing to know everything, and knowing nothing at all. On account of this obstinacy of theirs, understanding departed from them, and foolish senselessness entered into them. And they praise themselves as having wisdom, and desire to become teachers, although destitute of sense. On account, therefore, of this loftiness of mind,

many became vain, exalting themselves: for self-will and empty
confidence is a great demon. Of these, accordingly, many were
rejected, but some repented and believed, and subjected themselves to those that had understanding, knowing their own foolishness. And to the rest of this class repentance is open; for they
were not wicked, but rather foolish, and without understanding. If
these therefore repent, they will live unto God; but if they do not
repent, they shall have their dwelling with the women who wrought
wickedness among them."

Chapter 23

"And those from the sixth mountain, which had clefts large and
small, and decayed grass in the clefts, who believed, were the following: they who occupy the small clefts are those who bring
charges against one another, and by reason of their slanders have
decayed in the faith. Many of them, however, repented; and the
rest also will repent when they hear my commandments, for
their slanders are small, and they will quickly repent. But they
who occupy the large clefts are persistent in their slanders, and
vindictive in their anger against each other. These, therefore, were
thrown away from the tower, and rejected from having a part in
its building. Such persons, accordingly, shall have difficulty in
living. If our God and Lord, who rules over all things, and has
power over all His creation, does not remember evil against those
who confess their sins, but is merciful, does man, who is corruptible and full of sins, remember evil against a fellow-man, as if he

were able to destroy or to save him? I, the angel of repentance, say unto you, As many of you as are of this way of thinking, lay it aside, and repent, and the Lord will heal your former sins, if you purify yourselves from this demon; but if not, you will be delivered over to him for death."

Chapter 24

"And those who believed from the seventh mountain, on which the grass was green and flourishing, and the whole of the mountain fertile, and every kind of cattle and the fowls of heaven were feeding on the grass on this mountain, and the grass on which they pastured became more abundant, were the following: they were always simple, and harmless, and blessed, bringing no charges against one another, but always rejoicing greatly because of the servants of God, and being clothed with the holy spirit of these virgins, and always having pity on every man, and giving aid from their own labour to every man, without reproach and without hesitation. The Lord, therefore, seeing their simplicity and all their meekness, multiplied them amid the labours of their hands, and gave them grace in all their doings. And I, the angel of repentance, say to you who are such, Continue to be such as these, and your seed will never be blotted out; for the Lord has made trial of you, and inscribed you in the number of us, and the whole of your seed will dwell with the Son of God; for ye have received of His Spirit."

Chapter 25

"And they who believed from the eighth mountain, where were the many fountains, and where all the creatures of God drank of the fountains, were the following: apostles, and teachers, who preached to the whole world, and who taught solemnly and purely the word of the Lord, and did not at all fall into evil desires, but walked always in righteousness and truth, according as they had received the Holy Spirit. Such persons, therefore, shall enter in with the angels."

Chapter 26

"And they who believed from the ninth mountain, which was deserted, and had in it creeping things and wild beasts which destroy men, were the following: they who had the stains as servants, who discharged their duty ill, and who plundered widows and orphans of their livelihood, and gained possessions for themselves from the ministry, which they had received. If, therefore, they remain under the dominion of the same desire, they are dead, and there is no hope of life for them; but if they repent, and finish their ministry in a holy manner, they shall be able to live. And they who were covered with scabs are those who have denied their Lord, and have not returned to Him again; but becoming withered and desert-like, and not cleaving to the servants of God, but living in solitude, they destroy then-own souls. For as a vine, when left within an enclosure, and meeting with neglect, is destroyed, and is made desolate by the weeds, and in time grows wild, and is no longer of any use to its master, so also are such men as have given themselves up, and become useless to their Lord, from having contracted savage habits. These men, therefore, have repentance in their power, unless they are found to have denied from the heart; but if any one is found to have denied from the heart, I do not know if he may live. And I say this not for these present days, in order that any one who has denied may obtain repentance, for it is impossible for him to be saved who now intends to deny his Lord; but to those who denied Him long ago, repentance seems to be possible. If, therefore, any one intends to repent, let him do so quickly, before the tower is completed; for if not, he will be utterly destroyed by the women. And the chipped stones are the deceitful and the slanderers; and the wild beasts which you saw on the ninth mountain, are the same. For as wild beasts destroy and kill a man by their poison, so also do the words of such men destroy and ruin a man. These, accordingly, are mutilated in their faith, on account of the deeds which they have done in themselves; yet some repented, and were saved. And the rest, who are of such a character, can be saved if they repent; but if they do not repent, they will perish with those women, whose strength they have assumed."

Chapter 27

"And from the tenth mountain, where were trees which over-shadowed certain sheep, they who believed were the following: bishops given to hospitality, who always gladly received into their houses the servants of God, without dissimulation. And the bishops never failed to protect, by their service, the widows, and those who were in want, and always maintained a holy conversation. All these, accordingly, shall be protected by the Lord for ever. They who do these things are honourable before God, and their place is already with the angels, if they remain to the end serving God."

Chapter 28

"And from the eleventh mountain, where were trees full of fruits, adorned with fruits of various kinds, they who believed were the following: they who suffered for the name of the Son of God, and who also suffered cheerfully with their whole heart, and laid down their lives." "Why, then, sir," I said, "do all these trees bear fruit, and some of them fairer than the rest?" "Listen," he said: "all who once suffered for the name of the Lord are honourable before God; and of all these the sins were remitted, because they suffered for the name of the Son of God. And why their fruits are of various kinds, and some of them superior, listen. All," he continued, "who were brought before the authorities and were examined, and did not deny, but suffered cheerfully—these are held in greater honour with God, and of these the fruit is superior; but all who were cowards, and in doubt, and who reasoned in their hearts whether they would deny or confess, and yet suffered, of these the fruit is less, because that suggestion came into their hearts; for that suggestion—that a servant should deny his Lord—

is evil. Have a care, therefore, ye who are planning such things, lest that suggestion remain in your hearts, and ye perish unto God. And ye who suffer for His name ought to glorify God, because He deemed you worthy to bear His name, that all your sins might be healed. [Therefore, rather deem yourselves happy], and think that ye have done a great thing, if any of you suffer on account of God. The Lord bestows upon you life, and ye do not understand, for your sins were heavy; but if you had not suffered for the name of the Lord, ye would have died to God on account of your sins. These things I say to you who are hesitating about denymg or confessing: acknowledge that ye have the Lord, lest, denying Him, ye be delivered up to prison. If the heathen chastise their slaves, when one of them denies his master, what, think ye, will your Lord do, who has authority over all men? Put away these counsels out of your hearts, that you may live continually unto God."

Chapter 29

"And they who believed from the twelfth mountain, which was white, are the following: they are as infant children, in whose hearts no evil originates; nor did they know what wickedness is, but always remained as children. Such accordingly, without doubt, dwell in the kingdom of God, because they defiled in nothing the commandments of God; but they remained like children all the days of their life in the same mind. All of you, then, who shall remain stedfast, and be as children, without doing evil, will be more honoured than all who have been previously mentioned; for all infants are honourable before God, and are the first persons with Him. Blessed, then, are ye who put away wickedness from yourselves, and put on innocence. As the first of all will you live unto God."

After he had finished the similitudes of the mountains, I said to him, "Sir, explain to me now about the stones that were taken out of the plain, and put into the building instead of the stones that were taken out of the tower; and about the round stones that were put into the building; and those that still remain round."

Chapter 30

"Hear," he answered, "about all these also. The stones taken out of the plain and put into the building of the tower instead of those that were rejected, are the roots of this white mountain. When, therefore, they who believed from the white mountain were all found guileless, the Lord of the tower commanded those from the roots of this mountain to be cast into the building of the tower; for he knew that if these stones were to go to the building of the tower, they would remain bright, and not one of them become black. But if he had so resolved with respect to the other mountains, it would have been necessary for him to visit that tower again, and to cleanse it. Now all these persons were found white who believed, and who will yet believe, for they are of the same race. This is a happy race, because it is innocent. Hear now, further, about these round and shining stones. All these also are from the white mountain. Hear, moreover, why they were found round: because their riches had obscured and darkened them a little from the truth, although they never departed from God; nor did any evil word proceed out of their mouth, but all justice, virtue, and truth. When the Lord, therefore, saw the mind of these persons, that they were born good, and could be good, He ordered their riches to be cut down, not to be taken away for ever, that they might be able to do some good with what was left them; and they will live unto God, because they are of a good race. Therefore were they rounded a little by the chisel, and put in the building of the tower.

Chapter 31

"But the other round stones, which had not yet been adapted to the building of the tower, and had not yet received the seal, were for this reason put back into their place, because they are exceedingly round. Now this age must be cut down in these things, and in the vanities of their riches, and then they will meet in the kingdom of God; for they must of necessity enter into the kingdom of God, because the Lord has blessed this innocent race. Of this race, therefore, no one will perish; for although any of them be tempted by the most wicked devil, and commit sin, he will quickly return to his Lord. I deem you happy, I, who am the messenger of repentance, whoever of you are innocent as children, because your part is good, and honourable before God. Moreover, I say to you all, who have received the seal of the Son of God, be clothed with simplicity, and be not mindful of offences, nor remain in wickedness. Lay aside, therefore, the recollection of your offences and bitternesses, and you will be formed in one spirit. And heal and take away from you those wicked schisms, that if the Lord of the flocks come, He may rejoice concerning you. And He will rejoice, if He find all things sound, and none of you shall perish. But if He find any one of these sheep strayed, woe to the shepherds! And if the shepherds themselves have strayed, what answer will they give Him for their flocks? Will they perchance say that they were harassed by their flocks? They will not be believed, for the thing is incredible that a shepherd could suffer from his flock; rather will he be punished on account of his falsehood. And I myself am a shepherd, and I am under a most stringent necessity of rendering an account of you."

Chapter 32

"Heal yourselves, therefore, while the tower is still building. The Lord dwells in men that love peace, because He loved peace; but from the contentious and the utterly wicked He is far distant. Restore to Him, therefore, a spirit sound as ye received it. For when you have given to a fuller a new garment, and desire to receive it back entire at the end, if, then, the fuller return you a torn garment, will you take it from him, and not rather be angry, and abuse him, saying, 'I gave you a garment that was entire: why have you rent it, and made it useless, so that it can be of no use on account of the rent which you have made in it?' Would you not say all this to the fuller about the rent which you found in your garment? If, therefore, you grieve about your garment, and complain because you have not received it entire, what do you think the Lord will do to you, who gave you a sound spirit, which you have rendered altogether useless, so that it can be of no service to its possessor? for its use began to be unprofitable, seeing it was corrupted by you. Will not the Lord, therefore, because of this conduct of yours regarding His Spirit, act in the same way, and deliver you over to death? Assuredly, I say, he will do the same to all those whom He shall find retaining a recollection of offences. Do not trample His mercy under foot, He says, but rather honour Him, because He is so patient with your sins, and is not as ye are. Repent, for it is useful to you."

Chapter 33

"All these things which are written above, I, the Shepherd, the messenger of repentance, have showed and spoken to the servants of God. If therefore ye believe, and listen to my words, and walk in them, and amend your ways, you shall have it in your power to live: but if you remain in wickedness, and in the recollection of offences, no sinner of that class will live unto God. All these words which I had to say have been spoken unto you."

The Shepherd said to me, "Have you asked me everything?" And I replied, "Yes, sir." "Why did you not ask me about the shape of the stones that were put into the building, that I might explain to you why we filled up the shapes?" And I said, "I forgot, sir." "Hear now, then," he said, "about this also. These are they who have now heard my commandments, and repented with their whole hearts. And when the Lord saw that their repentance was good and pure, and that they were able to remain in it, He ordered their former sins to be blotted out. For these shapes were their sins, and they were levelled down, that they might not appear."

Tenth Similitude
Concerning Repentance
and Alms-Giving

∾

Chapter 1

AFTER I HAD FULLY written down this book, that messenger
who had delivered me to the Shepherd came into the house in
which I was, and sat down upon a couch, and the Shepherd stood
on his right hand. He then called me, and spoke to me as follows:
"I have delivered you and your house to the Shepherd, that you
may be protected by him." "Yes, sir," I said. "If you wish, therefore, to be protected," he said, "from all annoyance, and from all
harsh treatment, and to have success in every good work and
word, and to possess all the virtues of righteousness, walk in
these commandments which he has given you, and you will be
able to subdue all wickedness. For if you keep those commandments, every desire and pleasure of the world will be subject to
you, and success will attend you in every good work. Take unto

yourself his experience and moderation, and say to all that he is in great honour and dignity with God, and that he is a president with great power, and mighty in his office. To him alone throughout the whole world is the power of repentance assigned. Does he seem to you to be powerful? But you despise his experience, and the moderation which he exercises towards you."

Chapter 2

I said to him, "Ask himself, sir, whether from the time that he has entered my house I have done anything improper, or have offended him in any respect." He answered, "I also know that you neither have done nor will do anything improper, and therefore I speak these words to you, that you may persevere. For he had a good report of you to me, and you will say these words to others, that they also who have either repented or will still repent may entertain the same feelings with you, and he may report well of these to me, and I to the Lord." And I said, "Sir, I make known to every man the great works of God: and I hope that all those who love them, and have sinned before, on hearing these words, may repent, and receive life again." "Continue, therefore, in this ministry, and finish it. And all who follow out his commands shall have life, and great honour with the Lord. But those who do not keep his commandments, flee from his life, and despise him. But he has his own honour with the Lord. All, therefore, who shall despise him, and not follow his commands, deliver themselves to death, and every one of them will be guilty of his own blood. But I enjoin you, that you obey his commands, and you will have a cure for your former sins."

Chapter 3

"Moreover, I sent you these virgins, that they may dwell with you. For I saw that they were courteous to you. You will therefore have them as assistants, that you may be the better able to keep his commands: for it is impossible that these commandments can be observed without these virgins. I see, moreover, that they abide with you willingly; but I will also instruct them not to depart at all from your house: do you only keep your house pure, as they will delight to dwell in a pure abode. For they are pure, and chaste, and industrious, and have all influence with the Lord. Therefore, if they find your house to be pure, they will remain with you; but if any defilement, even a little, befall it, they will immediately withdraw from your house. For these virgins do not at all like any defilement." I said to him, "I hope, sir, that I will please them, so that they may always be willing to inhabit my house. And as he to whom you entrusted me has no complaint against me, so neither will they have." He said to the Shepherd, "I see that the servant of God wishes to live, and to keep these commandments, and will place these virgins in a pure habitation." When he had spoken these words he again delivered me to the Shepherd, and called those virgins, and said to them, "Since I see that you are willing to dwell in his house, I commend him and his house to you, asking that you withdraw not at all from it." And the virgins heard these words with pleasure.

Chapter 4

The angel then said to me, "Conduct yourself manfully in this service, and make known to every one the great things of God, and you will have favour in this ministry. Whoever, therefore, shall walk in these commandments, shall have life, and will be happy in his life; but whosoever shall neglect them shall not have life, and will be unhappy in this life. Enjoin all, who are able to act rightly, not to cease well-doing; for, to practice good works is useful to them. And I say that every man ought to be saved from inconveniences. For both he who is in want, and he who suffers inconveniences in his daily life, is in great torture and necessity. Whoever, therefore, rescues a soul of this kind from necessity, will gain for himself great joy. For he who is harassed by inconveniences of this kind, suffers equal torture with him who is in chains. Moreover many, on account of calamities of this sort, when they could not endure them, hasten their own deaths. Whoever, then, knows a calamity of this kind afflicting a man, and does not save him, commits a great sin, and becomes guilty of his blood. Do good works, therefore, ye who have received good from the Lord; lest, while ye delay to do them, the building of the tower be finished, and you be rejected from the edifice: there is now no other tower a-building. For on your account was the work of building suspended. Unless, then, you make haste to do rightly, the tower will be completed, and you will be excluded."

After he had spoken with me he rose up from the couch, and taking the Shepherd and the virgins, he departed. But he said to me that he would send back the Shepherd and the virgins to my dwelling. Amen.

REDISCOVER THESE TIMELESS CLASSICS!
Moody Classics

MOODY
PUBLISHERS.

1-800-678-8812   MOODYPUBLISHERS.COM